热爱生命

—— Love of Life ——

吴子劲 著

Billson International Ltd.

Published by
Billson International Ltd
27 Old Gloucester Street
London
WC1N 3AX
Tel:(852)95619525

Website:www.billson.cn
E-mail address:cs@billson.cn

First published 2025

Produced by Billson International Ltd
CDPF/01

ISBN 978-1-80377-155-7

©Hebei Zhongban Culture Development Co.,Ltd All rights reserved.

The original content within this product remains the property of Hebei Zhongban Culture Development Co.,Ltd, and cannot be reproduced without prior permission. Updates and derivative works of the original content remain the property of Hebei Zhongban. and are provided by Hebei Zhongban Culture Development Co.,Ltd.

The authors and publisher have made every attempt to ensure that the information contained in this book is complete, accurate and true at the time of printing. You are invited to provide feedback of any errors, omissions and suggestions for improvement.

Every attempt has been made to acknowledge copyright. However, should any infringement have occurred, the publisher invites copyright owners to contact the address below.

Hebei Zhongban Culture Development Co.,Ltd
Wanda Office Building B, 215 Jianhua South Street, Yuhua District, Shijiazhuang City, Hebei province, 2207

目 录
Contents

剑龙与竹子的情书，惊艳了岁月
Jianlong and bamboo love letter, amazing years

引子	2
intro	3
后记	135
Postscript	137

一个抑郁症患者的手记
Notes of a depressed patient

前言	142
Foreword	157
我与严重的抑郁症，顽强搏斗手记之一	177
I struggle with severe depression, tenacious notes 1	181
我与严重的抑郁症，顽强搏斗手记之二	186
I struggle with severe depression, tenacious notes 2	189
我与严重的抑郁症，顽强搏斗手记之三	193
I struggle with severe depression, tenacious notes 3	195

我与严重的抑郁症，顽强搏斗手记之四	198
I struggle with severe depression, tenacious notes 4	200
我与严重的抑郁症，顽强搏斗手记之五	202
I struggle with severe depression, tenacious notes 5	204
我与严重的抑郁症，顽强搏斗手记之六	207
I struggle with severe depression, tenacious notes 6	208
我与严重的抑郁症，顽强搏斗手记之七	210
I struggle with severe depression, tenacious notes 7	211
我与严重的抑郁症，顽强搏斗手记之八	212
I struggle with severe depression, tenacious notes 8	213
我与严重的抑郁症，顽强搏斗手记之九	215
I struggle with severe depression, tenacious notes 9	218

我的作品
My works

雄鹰之歌	224
Song of the Eagle	228
我的父母亲	232
My parents	238
春风吹又生	247
Spring breeze blows again	250
秋日的私语	254
Whispers of Autumn	256
雕刻时光	258
Carving Time	260

剑龙与竹子的情书，惊艳了岁月

Jianlong and bamboo love letter, amazing years

引子

那年的一个秋夜。

剑龙送走客户，回到香港中环广场写字楼。

落地玻璃窗外，维多利亚港两岸灯火辉煌，错落有致的高厦星光熠熠，处处吐露东方之珠的璀璨繁华。

他坐在转椅上，儒雅的脸庞陷入沉思。

他目光落在一封信上——离婚判决书，这几个字如五雷轰顶，阵阵痛楚撕心裂肺，他禁不住喃喃自语："竹子，我俩真的缘尽于此？"

谁能明白，刚刚还和客户杯斛相碰把酒言欢的他，此刻却凝视静静的海面，眼角一滴泪悄然滑落。

十七年呵，十七年相识相知相亲相爱，终究敌不过生活的巨掌，怎不令人唏嘘不已？

剑龙打开书桌锁上多时的抽屉，取出两本厚厚的尘封多时的日记，那一页页笔录的情笺如流光轻舞，那些刻骨铭心的旧时光，再次揭开他与竹子尘封的往事与记忆。

intro

One autumn night that year.

Jianlong sent away customers and returned to the Hong Kong Central Plaza office building.

Outside the floor-to-ceiling glass window, the two sides of Victoria Harbour are brightly lit, and the scattered high- buildings are star-studded, revealing the brilliance and prosperity of the Pearl of the Orient.

He sat in his swivel chair, his refined face lost in thought.

His eyes fell on a letter-the divorce verdict. These words were like five thunderstorms, and the pain tore his heart and lungs. He couldn't help muttering to himself: "Bamboo, we are really here?"

Who can understand, just also and customer cup Hu meet to drink happy him, but at the moment staring at the quiet sea, the corner of his eye 1 tears quietly sliding down.

Seventeen years, seventeen years of acquaintance, mutual understanding and love, after all, but the giant palm of life, why not make people sad?

Jianlong opened the locked drawer of his desk for a long time and took out two thick dusty diaries. The notes of the pages of records like streamers and light dancing. Those unforgettable old times once again revealed his dust-laden past and memories with bamboo.

竹子：

　　想你，在绵绵雨中。

　　一月底那晚相约在电话旁，焦灼等待了一小时，没你音讯，十分惆怅。

　　此后，想你离乡别井，在繁华的香港，也许就此隔别了，不觉凄然若失，若有所悲。

　　以为你到香港会来信，期盼着，但别来三个多月都在失望中。

　　三个月在香港，未知你可定下去向？怕你从此他乡孤旅，你一个纤纤女子可承受得了孤苦无依。

　　香港的喧嚣及人情的冷暖时有所闻，但始终相信人心总有天良。

　　喜欢捧读席慕蓉的诗集，三本不太厚的集子，来回轻吟寻味，那样温馨，蕴含淡淡的哀伤无奈，却又如此深刻如此柔情似水。梁实秋的《雅舍小品》，亦庄亦谐，妙趣横生，是一本很难得的书。

　　对书真是一种与生俱来，生死与共的铭心之爱，只恨不成书痴，而免遍染世俗的尘埃。

　　有空请来信说说你的近况，好续你我的缘分。

　　虽不曾伴你同行，而心灵不也时时因交流而撞出灿烂的火花？

竹子珍重

剑龙

4月8日

Bamboo:

　　Miss you, in the rain.

　　At the end of January, I met by the phone that night. I waited anxiously for an hour. I didn't any news from you. I was very disappointed.

Since then, I want you to leave your hometown. In the prosperous Hong Kong, you may be separated from each other. I feel sad and if you have any.

I thought you would write to Hong Kong and look forward to it, but don't be disappointed for more than 3 month.

3 month in Hong Kong, I don't know where you can go? I'm afraid you can alone from now on. You, a slender woman, can bear the loneliness and hardship.

We have heard of the hustle and bustle of Hong Kong and the warmth and warmth of human feelings from time to time, but we always believe that there is always a conscience in the hearts of the people.

I like to read Xi Murong's poems, three collections that are not too thick, and I chant and pondered back and forth. It is so warm and contains a touch of sadness and helplessness, but it is so profound and tender. Liang Shiqiu's "elegant house sketch", also Zhuang also harmonious, witty, is a very rare book.

1 is really a kind of innate love for books, the common of life and death, only hate not books crazy, but avoid worldly dust.

Please write and tell me about your recent situation when you are free, so as to continue your fate.

Although I have never accompanied you, and my heart is not, I always have brilliant sparks due to communication?

Take care of bamboo

Jianlong

8 April

热爱生命
Love of Life

剑龙：

　　三个月前相约通电话，但在约定的时间里三次电话通了都没有人接，一恼之下，便不肯提笔给你写信，谁不知你亦以近似的理由，冷落了笔和信笺三个月，你呀你。

　　四月十四日中午，父母、表姐、表姐夫送我出门时，母亲信手打开信箱，拿起一封信，自言自语道：竹子小姐展。我一阵脸红，母亲将信递给我，信封上熟悉的笔迹令我惊喜。

　　途中展信细阅，惹得表姐夫呷干醋，认定我是在读情信，我告诉他，这是一个顶好顶好的朋友的来信，不是情信。

　　"无情不似多情苦，多情笑我枉用心"，情场上曾经失意的人，是不会再轻易把心抛出去的了。

　　我想，上天降临这许多的苦难在我身上，日后将会双倍偿还给我快乐。

　　香港三个月的生活，初步认识了这个繁华大都市的人情世态，并觉得颇合我这个女野心家的发展，至于"九七"问题，自信"车到山前必有路"。

　　数月不用笔，文字就生疏了许多。

　　"朝中有人好做官"自古皆然，我旧日的男朋友，就是因不满现状孤闯天涯去了，正是：生命诚可贵，爱情价更高，若为自由故，两者皆可抛。对此，我理解支持，但痛苦。婚姻对于中国女子的束缚太深，一失足成千古恨，再回头已成百年身。

　　　　　　　　　　　　　　　　　　祝好。

　　　　　　　　　　　　　　　　　　　竹子
　　　　　　　　　　　　　　　　　　4月19日

剑龙与竹子的情书，惊艳了岁月
Jianlong and bamboo love letter, amazing years

Jianlong:

I made an appointment to talk on the phone 3 months ago, but no one answered the phone three times within the appointed time. 1 annoyed, I refused to write to you. Who didn't know that you also snubbed the pen and letterhead for 3 months for similar reasons, you ah you.

At noon on April 14, when my parents, cousin and brother-in-law sent me out, my mother opened the mailbox, picked up a letter and said to herself, "miss bamboo exhibition. I blushed and my mother handed me the letter. The familiar handwriting on the envelope surprised me.

On the way, I and read the carefully the letter, which made my cousin's brother-in-law feel jealous and decided that I was reading love letter. I told him that this was a letter from a good friend, not a love letter.

"Ruthless is not like affectionate bitterness, affectionate laughter I waste heart", people who have been frustrated in love will not easily throw out their hearts.

I think that the many sufferings that heaven has brought upon me will be repaid to me twice in the future.

After 3 months of life in Hong Kong, I have a preliminary understanding of the human conditions of this prosperous metropolis, and feel that it is quite in line with the development of my careeress. As for the "1997" issue, I am confident that "there must be a way to get to the front of the mountain".

Months without a pen, the words are much rusty.

"There are people in the court who are good officials" has been around since ancient times. My old boyfriend went to the world alone because he was dissatisfied with the current situation. It is precisely: life is precious, love is more expensive, and if it is freedom, both can be thrown away. To this, I understand support, but pain. Marriage is too deeply bound to Chinese women, and it has become a for a hundred years to turn back.

Good luck.

Bamboo

19 April

竹子：

  咳好点了？

  记得你说过，每年都会有一次重感冒。

  今晚归家，翻开"文学报"，不经意发现"三毛回来了"的版面，很开心：久违了，三毛！

  几度沧桑，三毛依然故我，那率真的笑容，充满智慧的眸子，令人感叹其动人。

  读曹明华的作品，处处充满哲思，平实语言之中透出深刻的哲理。

  我喜欢自自然然，轻轻松松随意倾诉的朋友，一切如深谷中的涓流或是如山岗上那一轮静静的满月，平滑透明美丽如玉。

  我五月上旬会返家乡，身体不适归家调理，许多话，容我们见面时细说。

  兰姐可好？若有缘很快就可见面了，请代问安。

剑龙

4月20日

Bamboo:

Is your cough better?

Remember you said, every year will have a bad cold.

When I returned home tonight, I opened the "Literary Journal" and found the layout of "San Mao is back". I was very happy: long time no see, San Mao!

After several vicissitudes of life, San Mao is still the same as me. His frank smile and wise eyes make people sigh with emotion.

When you read the works of Cao Minghua, you are full of philosophical thoughts and profound philosophy is revealed in plain language.

I like friends who are natural and easy to talk to at will. Everything is like a trickle of in a deep valley or a quiet full moon on a mountain, smooth, transparent and beautiful as jade.

I will return to my hometown in early May. I will return home to recuperate when I feel unwell. Let's talk about many things in detail when we meet.

How is Lanjie? If you are destined to meet soon, please say hello.

Jianlong
20 April

剑龙君：

听到的依然是你柔和的嗓音，看到的依然是你温和微笑的心灵，依然如我心中欢唱的河流，我眼中绵延的草地，我梦中蔚蓝的海洋。

夜朦胧、灯朦胧、情朦胧、人朦胧，这样的相对为何不是在从前？

第一次抑制不住汹涌的眼泪，一颗心，为着这不肯承认

热爱生命
Love of Life

的深深的爱。

我以为：早在那一个仿佛的黄昏，白瑞德已随风飘去。

佛说：修百世方能同舟，修行不深呵，现在你船上载着的是淡泊与宁静，我苦苦撑着的是利诱和功名，但是，总有一天我会卸下船上的货物，轻舟进行百世修炼，背道而驰的你我，也总有共聚重拾往事的一天，即使我已是白发苍苍的老妇，你已是苍苍白发的老翁。

刻骨相思缕心时，顿悟：最好的原是拥有一份期待，永恒的是泯灭不了的记忆，漫漫长夜里，能为你哭泣，凄凄风雨中能为你思念，笑容里为你祝福，悠悠百世，竟可以同样的绚丽。

第一次与你共舞，第一次这样激动胆怯——活脱脱的我，在你面前我柔顺无依，仿如迷途的羔羊，自信与豁达都交给了你。

想不到兰姐如此欣赏你，这正是我所盼。在我离开大陆的未来日子，你可会如我一样给她欢笑及鼓励？一位如此美丽多情而宽厚的女子，像你一样的情怀——恬淡宁静。

我希望所有的人都能如兰姐一样珍惜、敬重你，可是，相识天下，相知能几？

人生得一知己足矣。

如你这般以出世的精神处入世的事情，便能永远钟情于这个世界。

能相聚总是缘，我会好好珍惜你这份情谊。

请你保重。

竹子
1989 年 5 月 15 日

剑龙与竹子的情书，惊艳了岁月
Jianlong and bamboo love letter, amazing years

Jianlong :

What I hear is still your soft voice, what I see is still your gentle smiling heart, what I see is still the river singing in my heart, the grass in my eyes, the blue ocean in my dream.

The night is hazy, the light is hazy, the feeling is hazy, the person is hazy, this relative why not in the past?

For the first time, I can't restrain the surging tears, a heart, for this deep love that refuses to admit.

I thought: as early as in that one seemingly dusk, Rhett had gone with the wind.

Buddha said: Only when you practice for a hundred generations can you be in the same boat. Now your boat is carrying indifference and tranquility. What I am struggling to support is inducement and fame. However, one day I will unload the goods on the boat and practice for a hundred generations. You and I, who run counter to each other, will always gather together to regain the past. Even if I am a white-haired old woman, you are a white-haired old man.

When the heart of acacia, the epiphany: the best is to have a 1 expectation, the eternal is the memory that cannot be extinguished, the long night, can cry for you, the sad wind and rain can miss you, the smile can bless you, for a long time, can be the same gorgeous.

The first time I danced with you, the first time I was so excited and timid–I was alive, I was soft and unattached in front of you, like a lost lamb, and my confidence and open-mindedness were handed over to you.

I didn't expect LanJie to appreciate you so much. This is xactly what I looking forward. In the future days when I leave the mainland,

热爱生命
Love of Life

will you give her the same laughter and encouragement as I did? 1 such a beautiful and affectionate and generous woman, feelings like you –calm and quiet.

I hope all people can cherish and respect you like Lanjie. However, how many can we to know the world?

It is enough to have a confidant in life.

If you are and enter the world with the spirit of your birth, you will be able to love the world forever.

It is always to get together. I will cherish your friendship.

Please take care of yourself.

Bamboo
May 15, 1989

剑龙读了竹子这封表露心迹的信，颇费踌躇，不知该不该回信？拒绝一定会伤害竹子的心，不拒绝又不知会引致怎样的结果，怎么办？他试着沉默，希望竹子会明白他的心而将热情冷却。

假期一结束，剑龙便匆匆回到了珠海。

他打电话给兰姐问竹子的情形，她说竹子十分伤心，常常躲在房中默默无言，剑龙心中不安也不忍，便执笔写道：

Jianlong read this heart-revealing letter from bamboo and hesitated. I wonder if I should reply? Rejection will definitely hurt bamboo's heart. If you don't refuse, you don't know what kind of result it will lead to. What should you do? He tried to be silent, hoping that Bamboo would understand his heart and cool his enthusiasm.

1 the end of the holiday, the Jianlong hurried back to Zhuhai.

He called LanJie to ask about the situation of bamboo. She

said that bamboo was very sad and often hid in the room in silence. Jianlong felt uneasy and could not bear it. she wrote:

竹子：

可好？此刻执笔，恍如隔世。

我凝望窗前团团烟云，心绪何止万千！相聚情景如电影一样历历在目。

依然感觉到我俩如轻云舒卷，行云流水般的快步舞，依然感觉到水兵舞的狂放，感到你的战栗激动记得你脸颊的酡红。深深理解你爱我的情，得不到回应的苦和哀。那泪汩而出的伤泪，令我心酸。

明知道最好是同样回报，但我不能欺骗自己。

此刻你在做些什么？与兰姐相对共诉心事？谁人可解你心头无言的伤悲？

席慕蓉说：难道／青春必然愚昧／爱／必得忧伤？

竹子，这个假期，你虽表露了心迹，但我不能如你所想的接受，我只愿永远保有这份洁如夏荷的友谊。

诚然，在你面前我最自由自在，默默时有静对的和谐，高歌时有共醉的心神，吟诵诗歌时共鸣的意境，令人笑中有泪，泪中有笑，我俩相处，纵是言语不多，也能会心微笑。

这样的情谊，怎不令人感动？我非常珍惜彼此相处的每段时光，贯串它们如串珍珠，挂在记忆的颈项。

别后，何日再相逢？

返珠海我又要做一番努力，好完成积压多时的工作。

竹子珍重
剑龙
1989 年 6 月 11 日

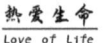
Love of Life

Bamboo:

Okay? Writing at the moment is like a lifetime ago.

I stared at the window a cloud of smoke, more than a thousand thoughts! The meeting was as vivid as a movie.

I still feel that we are like light clouds and light clouds and light clouds and flowing water. I still feel the wild release of the sailor dance. I feel your trembling and excited. I remember the flush of your cheeks. Deep understanding of your love for me, the pain and of not getting a response. That of gurgling injury tears, make me sad.

Knowing that the best is the same return, but I can't deceive myself.

What are you doing at the moment? and LanJie relative common complaints? Who can relieve the silent sorrow in your heart?

Xi Murong said: Is it true that youth must be foolish/love/sorrow?

Bamboo, this holiday, although you have shown your heart, but I can't accept it as you think. I only wish to keep this and clean like Xia and lotus friendship forever.

Admittedly, I am the freest in front of you. I have the harmony of quietness and in silence. I have the to drunk mind when singing. The artistic conception that resonates when reciting poems makes people laugh with tears and laugh with tears. Even if we don't speak much, we can smile with understanding.

How can such a friendship not be touched? I cherish every time I get along with each other, through them like a string of pearls, hanging on the neck of memory.

When will we meet again?

When I return to Zhuhai, I will make another effort to finish the long backlog of work.

Take care of bamboo

Jianlong

June 11, 1989

就这样,剑龙和竹子又频繁通起信来。
In this way, Jianlong and bamboo and frequent communication.

剑龙:

寂寞有时是一种异常美的境界。

灯下,独自翻阅这颗寂寞的心——那爱换来的寂寞,仿佛昨夜星辰,闪烁不灭!

不知想什么,不知能写什么,揉成一团团的稿纸,可述说得了那乱纷纷的心?不敢言苦这是上苍的安排。

读你十一日来信,感觉是不堪回首,意志坚强,感情脆弱的我,多希望给你一抹微笑,可字字句句,伤泪斑斑。

龙应台是个女作家、女哲人、女博士,我为什么不可以是富家少奶先生贤妻?为何要笑傲江湖游戏人生心在流浪魂在异乡漂泊?为何扑进粉红色陷阱,临溪汲饮后还要带水上路却言"自由价更高"?为何"待海枯到可烂,天地合,乃敢与君绝?"为何宠辱不惊,看庭前花开花落,去留无意,看天上云卷云舒?

不会挽留你决意远离的脚步,不会奢望你的目光永远专注于我,也许徐志摩的"偶然"一诗很残酷,但是,你记得也好,最好你忘掉,这交汇时互放的光亮!

时值凌晨,没月色,漫蒙无边的黑夜里,只有我临窗一盏灯,远处传来小孩的哭声,划破夜的宁静。

此刻你在做什么？梦里？书乡？海天遐想中？

今夜风很清凉，看窗台上碧绿的富贵竹，思念你久违了一个月的花花草草，可是"绿肥红瘦"？望书架上怡然躺着的伙伴，不知你的宝贝是否别来无恙？老友阿刚可好？

天地万物，包括至灵至圣的人类，能有缘分几许？你我由最初的相识，到今日的相知，足足用九年的时间，茫茫人海之中噢，为何刚相聚又要分离？也许天是无情的，因此永不老去，多情的男女，却经不起岁月的摧磨！

是到了最后告别的时刻了，剑龙，若果他日你爱上了我的姐妹，宽厚地待她吧。

水兵舞的狂放，慢华尔兹的轻柔，探戈的胆怯都已经贡献给了你，酡红、颤抖、汩汩而出的清泪也献给了你，孩子气、任性、傻劲也在你面前表露无遗，知否？你是我不装饰的镜子。

生活的苦难，使我学会了感激，拥有的，便是最好！

不要怕爱的绳索将你套住，你还是水般澄澈，风般飞扬，你依然拥有诗人般浪漫的气质，都市人现实的内心。

今天去收发室翻找，当看到熟悉的信封，信封上熟悉的字迹，心中竟有着轰然的狂喜，回到办公室，低下头在抽屉里读信，更有莫名的激动，中午下班回到宿舍见到兰姐，竟甜甜地叫了她一声，却欲言又止，拿出录音带坐在地上听你唱的歌，泪水就在不知不觉之中流了下来……

晚上哼着歌，用力拖地板，抹地胶，擦桌子，洗干净那一篮花，为富贵竹洒上清水，洗完澡后换上清爽的睡衣，拧开台灯在桌前给你写信。

不知什么教我忘形，不知什么令我快乐，多日积累的凄苦，烦闷中竟有一份欣慰。

我是经不起诱惑的呵，求你不要再用你的柔情，安抚这颗失落的心。

兰姐当年也曾拥有一个地老天荒的故事：在故乡财校读书时，每周三，总收到一封来自中大的厚厚的信，每当忆起那份等待情信的幸福紧张时，一如当年那个美丽清纯的少女。后来，由于误会，由于各自的骄傲，她嫁了人，男朋友至今未娶，回首当年，才知道骄傲的愚昧。

嫁一个男人或娶一个女子是件容易的事，但要结束一桩婚姻却是会耗尽心神，耗尽人生的热情和乐趣。因此曾去信劝告阿娟，不要违背自己的衷曲下嫁而误了未来的岁月，她在犹豫之中。

言及此，记起一个女子在沙漠上的故事——

一望无际的沙漠上，一素装的女子在独行，唇已经渴得干裂，身姿如风摆的杨柳显得如此柔弱无依，驻足翘首时，看到不远处有一只杯子，欣喜若狂地走上前去，但杯却是空的，失望几乎将她击倒，她跪在地上，哀怨地望着上苍，泪水涟涟，也不知道过了多久，才带着一颗受怆的心上路。

如此默默地走啊走，独自承受了诉不完的孤苦艰辛，向着遥远不可知的前方走去。

突然，灰蒙蒙的沙漠上，展现一片绿荫，一汪清泉，这女子几乎不敢相信自己的眼睛，怔怔地注视着汩汩而流的泉水，感激地哭了，缓缓地弯下腰，捧起清泉，渗着泪水喝了下去，然后带着水，依依不舍地走下去。

也不知走了多久，沙漠上出现了一座小屋，这女子犹豫地停下脚步，心在祈祷：但愿屋里有充饥的饭菜，干净的床铺和一位慈善的老奶奶，可是，开门的却是一位年轻英俊的男子，他温柔怜爱的目光抚慰了这位憔悴的女子，一刹那间，这

> 女子几乎失去了走下去的勇气，然而，她仍是谢了主人的挽留，带着疲倦的身心和淡然的微笑，跨了过去。
>
> 终于看到了城墙，但那却是没有门的城墙，隔着墙壁，依稀听到了里面传来车马的喧声，这女子却倚着城墙倒了下去……
>
> 竹子不忍再写下去了。

案安！

竹子

1989年6月28日

Jianlong:

  Loneliness is sometimes 1 a state of extraordinary beauty.

  Under the lamp, read this lonely heart alone- the loneliness that love exchange, as if the stars last night, twinkling!

  I don't know what to think, I don't know what to write, I can tell the heart of chaos? Dare not say bitter this is God's arrangement.

  Reading your letter on the 11th of the, I feel unbearable, strong-willed and emotionally fragile. I hope to give you a smile. I can every word in my and hurt tears and stains.

  Long Yingtai is a female writer, philosopher and doctor. Why can't I be the good wife of Mr. from a rich family with little milk? Why do you want the legendary swordsman to play the game, the heart is wandering, the soul is wandering in a foreign land and? Why do you jump into the trap of pink and take water on the road after drinking in Linxi, but say that "the price of freedom is higher"? Why did "the of the sea withered to rotten, the heaven and the earth were together, but we dared to fight with you?" Why did we not be surprised, watching the flowers bloom and fall in front of the court, whether to stay or not, and watching the clouds and clouds in the sky?

I will not detain the steps you are determined to stay away from, and I will not expect your eyes to focus on me forever. Perhaps Xu Zhimo's poem "Accidental" is cruel, but if you remember it, you'd better forget it, the light that put on each other when they meet!

It was early in the morning, there was no moonlight, in the boundless night, only I 1 a lamp near the window, and the cry of a child in the distance cut through the peace of the night.

What are you doing at the moment? In the dream? book township? In the sea and sky reverie?

The wind is very cool tonight. Look at the green and rich bamboo on the windowsill. I miss the flowers and plants you have not seen for a month, but "green manure, red thin"? looking at partner lying on the bookshelf, I wonder if your baby is all right? How's my old friend Gang?

How can all things in heaven and earth, including the most spiritual the most holy human beings, the predestined? From the initial acquaintance to today's acquaintance, you and I have spent nine years in the vast sea of people. Oh, why do just get together and separate? Perhaps days is merciless, so never old, affectionate men and women, but can not stand the of years!

It's time to say goodbye, Jianlong. If you fall in love with my sister some day, treat her kindly.

The wild dance of sailors, the gentle slow waltz and the timidity of tango have all been contributed to you. The red, trembling and tears of gurgling are also dedicated to you. Childishness, willfulness and foolishness are also fully revealed in front of you, do you know? You

Love of Life

are the mirror I don't decorate.

The suffering of life, so that I learned to appreciate, have, is the best!

Don't be afraid that the rope of love will trap you. You are still clear as water and flying as wind. You still have the romantic temperament of a poet and the realistic heart of an urban person.

Today, I went to the mail room to search. When I saw the familiar envelope and the familiar handwriting on the envelope, I was full of ecstasy. When I went back to the office, I lowered my head to read the letter in the drawer. I was even more excited. When I came back from work at noon to see Lanjie in the dormitory, the called her 1 sweetly, but stopped speaking. I took out the tape and sat on the ground to listen to your song. Tears. Tears...

At night, I hummed a song, mop the floor hard, wipe the floor, wipe the table, wash the 1 basket flowers, sprinkle clear water on the rich bamboo, change into fresh pajamas after taking a bath, turn on the lamp and write to you at the table.

I don't know what to teach me to forget, I don't know what makes me happy, many days of accumulated misery, boredom has a gratification.

I can't stand the temptation, please don't use your tenderness to appease this lost heart.

Lan Jie also had a story of the end of the world in those days: when she was studying in her hometown of school, she always received a thick letter from cuhk every Wednesday. whenever she remembered the happiness and tension of waiting for letter, she was just like the beautiful and pure girl in those days. Later, due to misunderstanding, due to their pride, she married someone, her boyfriend has not married, looking back on that year, only to know the ignorance of pride.

It is easy to marry a man or a woman, but to end 1 marriage is to exhaust the mind and the enthusiasm and pleasure of life. Therefore, she once sent a letter to advise Ah Juan not to go against her heart and marry down and miss the future years. She was hesitating.

I remember the story of a woman in the desert--

In the endless desert, 1 plain woman was walking alone, her lips were chapped with thirst, and the willow, whose posture was like the wind, looked so weak and helpless. When she stopped to look up, she saw a cup not far away and walked forward with ecstasy, but the cup was empty. Disappointment almost knocked her down. She knelt on the ground and looked sadly at the sky with tears. She didn't know how long it had been, only with 1 heart by the pathos on the road.

He walked silently and alone, endured endless hardships and hardships, and walked towards the distant and unknown front.

Suddenly, on the gray desert, there was a shade of green, 1 Wang Qingquan. The woman could hardly believe her eyes. She stared at the and flowing spring water, cried gratefully, bent down slowly, picked up the spring, drank it with tears, and then walked down reluctantly with the water.

I don't know how long it took to walk, 1 hut appeared in the desert. The woman stopped hesitantly, praying with her heart: I hope there are food, clean bed and a charitable old woman in the house. However, it was 1 young and handsome man who opened the door. His gentle and loving eyes comforted the gaunt woman and 1 the instant of, the woman almost lost the courage to go on, however, she still thanked the master's retention, with a tired body and mind and indifferent smile, across the past.

Finally, I saw the of the wall of the city, but it was the of the wall of the city without a door. across the wall of the wall, I vaguely heard the noise of horses and horses coming from inside, but the woman leaned against the of the wall of the city and fell down...

Bamboo can't bear to write anymore.

Ann case!

Bamboo

June 28, 1989

竹子：

　　这段时间，我心中思想的挣扎，情理的煎熬，何去何从的选择和取舍，令人百感交集。

　　理智告诉我，我俩之间是一段没有结果的爱，因为选择你，我必须抛弃自己赖以生存的事业，而我们一切的磨难会因此而起。

　　去国赴港已是你无可挽回的抉择，我没有你的条件，即使有，我也难于抛下事业，背井离乡浪迹天涯，作为一个男子，我应保有我自己的事业，而非依赖和仰仗他人而生存，因为这会伤害我做人的尊严，毁了我生活的宁静和幸福，我一直痛恨寄人篱下的生活。

　　我一方面想不顾一切去爱，一方面又洒脱不了，抛开已经有好发展的事业，而置生命于漂泊无定之中，我很彷徨。

　　竹子噢，爱你，却不能成为你终身的伴侣；放弃你，则葬送了一段深情，凄楚缠绵，思念一生，但是我们不得不——长别离。

还是理智些吧，念我俩都要食人间烟火，让彼此回复从前心如止水的境界，只要长留彼此于心间，则不枉我俩相识相知一场。

我知道，光有感情或过于理智的人生都是一种残缺，我只愿我心如水，珍藏对你的一切。

依依道珍重！

剑龙

1989年6月30日

Bamboo:

During this period of time, the struggle of my mind, the suffering of reason, the choice and choice of where to go, are mixed feelings.

Reason tells me that there is a fruitless love between us, because by choosing you, I must abandon the cause on which I live, and all our tribulations will result.

It is your irrevocable choice to go to Hong Kong. I don't have your conditions. Even if I do, it is difficult for me to leave my career and wander the world. As a man, I should keep my own career instead of relying on and relying on others to survive, because it will hurt my dignity as a human being and destroy the peace and happiness of my life. I have always hated the life under the fence.

On the one hand, I want to love regardless of everything, on the other hand, I can't be free and easy. I put aside the career that has been well developed and leave my life wandering. I am very hesitant.

Bamboo Oh, love you, but can not be your lifelong partner; give up you, then buried a deep feeling, sad lingering, miss life, but we have to-long parting.

Let's be rational, we both want to eat the fireworks, so that each other can return to the realm of before. As long as we stay in our hearts for a long time, we will not waste our 1 acquaintance.

I know that 1 is a kind of incomplete life that has feelings or is too rational. I only wish that my heart is like water and I treasure everything I have for you.

Yiyidao treasure!
Jianlong
June 30, 1989

剑龙：

明白你的心，也深知自由的价值。

如果我一大学毕业就去香港，如果去年到加拿大留学，我就不会懂得：爱是心甘情愿的无悔的给予。这份情升华了我的精神世界，虽然有不能相依的遗憾，但我无悔！

沉吟李清照的如梦令"常记溪亭日暮，沉醉不知归路，兴尽晚归舟，误入藕花深处，争渡争渡，惊起一滩鸥鹭。"这是一幅何等美妙动人的画卷？但以我这样的年纪，是不可以再拥有这份任性的了，而你的严谨，亦不会兴尽晚归，因而只能联想：夜下无人的沙滩上，风清月白波吟，情人间窃窃低语的温柔。

挣不脱这与生俱来的尘缘，今生，注定要在车马喧声之中行走，来世或可在峨眉山，觅一清静之所。

昨夜雨骤风疏，与兰姐对饮，仙泉清酿和香槟，一杯一杯地不胜酒力，却了悟，酒逢知己千杯少的喜悦，在人前我不饮酒，要醉，也只有醉倒在你和兰姐面前。

近日兰姐常提起旧情人，言语中流露出憧憬和无限温柔，十五年的相知，那份情早已根生于心，一时的误解和怨恨，忆起时依然只有美丽。

每次读你的信，都在庆幸你的文字与文章同样令人赏心悦目，刚毅有劲的落笔收笔，字句行间的紧凑有序，十分美丽，若在结构上再改善一下，则可以收到形神兼备之效。

今日为弟弟的女朋友阿玲写了一封情信，看她满心欢喜地离开，忽发奇想，当我老了，专剪辟一处静地，教少男少女写情信，你的信将是若干年后我执教时的素材，同时我不会如今天这般羞怯，对一班痴情的男女，可缓缓地讲述一个古老而美丽的爱情故事。

你给我的，实在是人间最珍贵的精神财富！

每日悠悠地等你的信，每次收信时仍是狂喜不已，永远无法深刻到不悲不喜的境界，记得"故乡行"的老奶奶吗？很喜欢她心中那份不泯的情愫。

时常这样伏案而写，不觉时光飞逝，每日守盼夜的来临，盼望在灯下用笔与你倾诉时的温柔。

纵使梦船将爱的希望全部载走，仍忘不了，属于你我的一切。

竹子

1989 年 7 月 18 日

Jianlong:

Know your heart and know the value of freedom.

If I had graduated from university in 1 and gone to Hong Kong, if I had studied in Canada last year, I would not have understood that love is given willingly and without regret. This feeling has sublimated my spiritual world. Although I have regrets that I cannot depend on each other, I have no regrets!

Li Qingzhao's dream-like order "always remember the sunset of the brook pavilion, intoxicated and not knowing the way back, returning to the boat at night, mistakenly into the depths of lotus flowers, fighting for crossing, startling gulls and herons on the 1 beach." What a wonderful and moving picture is this 1? However, at my age, I can no longer have this willfulness, and your rigor will not return late, so I can only associate: on the deserted beach at night, the wind and moon are white and the waves are and, and lovers whisper tenderness.

Earn not to get rid of this innate dust, this life, destined to walk in the noise of horses and horses, the next life or can be in the Emei Mountain, find a quiet place in the.

Last night, it rained suddenly and windy and. drank with Lanjie. Xianquan brewed and champagne. 1 cups and 1 cups were too strong to drink., it was to realize. It was a joy to meet friends for thousands of and a few cups. I didn't drink in front of people. I was drunk and, and only drunk in front of you and Lanjie.

Recently, Lanjie often mentions her old lover, and her words reveal longing and infinite tenderness. After 15 years of knowing each other, that love has long been rooted in her heart. A temporary misunderstanding and resentment are still only beautiful when she remembers it.

Every time I read your letter, I am glad that your words and articles are equally pleasing to the eye. I write with determination and strength. The lines are compact and orderly and very beautiful. If I improve the structure, I can get both form and spirit.

Today, I wrote a love letter for my younger brother's girlfriend, Arling. Seeing her leave happily, I suddenly had a whimsy. When I am old, I will cut a quiet place and teach boys and girls to write love letters. Your letter will be the material for me to teach in a few years' time. At the same time, I will not be as shy as today and infatuated with the men and women in 1 class, can slowly tell an old and beautiful love story.

What you gave me is really the most precious spiritual wealth in the world!

Waiting for your letter leisurely every day, every time I receive it, I am still ecstatic. I will never be able to go deep into the state of not being sad or happy. Do you remember the grandmother of "hometown trip? I like the feeling in her heart.

I often write at my desk like this, but I don't realize that time flies. I look forward to the coming of night every day, and I look forward to the gentleness when I talk to you with my pen under the lamp.

Even if the dream boat carry all the hopes of love, it still cannot forget everything that belongs to you and me.

Bamboo
18 July 1989

竹子：

对我这个无情的情人的守盼，可苦了你。

爱是人们心中一份执迷，其实是镜花水月，终归消散，世上真情传世的，亦不过只是短短的一瞬，茫茫人海之中，年轻的生命，有过心灵的颤动，虽是一刹，却成永恒。

永恒是心灵的感悟，是曾经心有所属的满足，是记忆画版上的不灭的印迹。

好文章是一种灵光的闪耀，文字并不代表承诺，评价一个人要看他真切的行动。

我不重承诺，一切随缘来去，时间可拿走的，随它去，

热爱生命
Love of Life

拿不走的自然根生于心。

人们都是由于急于去争取，故自背上了沉重的包袱，回首时，才惊觉原来这份重压完全是自找！

丰富的灵魂，总有不定的意绪，但智者将在每一次的憬悟之中，又向前飞跃一番，步步领略着人生，而言谈举止间亦更加气定神闲。

人生是一连串的叠印而成，每段经历的故事，都叠成今夜灿烂的星光。

我拥抱生活赐予我的幸与不幸，甜与苦，泪与笑。

依依道珍重。
剑龙
1989 年 7 月 23 日

Bamboo:

The of my heartless lover has hurt you.

Love is an obsession in people's hearts. In fact, it is a mirror and a moon in water. It will eventually dissipate. The true feelings in the world are only a short moment. In the vast sea of people, young life has had a spiritual tremor. Although it is 1, into eternity.

Eternity is the feeling of the soul, the satisfaction that the heart once belonged to, and the immortal imprint on the picture plate of memory.

A good article 1 a kind of spiritual sparkle. Words do not represent promises. The evaluation of a person depends on his real actions.

I don't re-promise, everything comes and goes with fate, time can take away, let it go, the natural roots that cannot be taken away born in the heart.

People are eager to fight for it, so they carry a heavy burden on their backs. When they look back, they are shocked to realize that this heavy pressure is completely self-seeking!

A rich soul always has an uncertain mood, but wise man will leap forward in every awakening, appreciate life step by step, and talk and behave more calmly.

Life is a series of superimposed, each experienced story, are folded into the brilliant starlight tonight.

I embrace the happiness and misfortune, sweet and bitter, tears and laughter that life has given me.

Yiyidao treasure.

Jianlong

23 July 1989

竹子：

念你醉里且贪欢笑，该醒了吧？这样大杯大杯地灌，醉仙李白也难胜任，你好任性！

我公司正进行岗位培训，大堆复习资料在桌上，却无心用功，只痴痴地沉入了相思。

风雨潇潇，夜正空蒙，凭窗远眺：云中谁寄锦书来？雁字回时，月满西楼，迢迢银汉，熠熠情星，知否柔情若水，佳期如梦？

志摩小曼的恋固然美丽，但志摩的早逝让人叹息。雨果及朱丽叶特的五十年生死恋，更是人间的千古绝唱！

微雨黄昏，微风独立，微言的人语以及微播的歌声，予我微醺的醉意，灯下絮语，越显温柔。

我如身处亭台，鸟瞰凝碧的海面，让目光的桨轻曼地划呀划呀，闻耳语：醉呵醉！

读过这首诗吗？

热爱生命
Love of Life

"你是正在旅行的一只候鸟
偶尔地
走访了我秋的园林
毫无顾惜地,你又自遥远了
遥远了远到不可知的天边
你去寻寻另一座春的园林吗
我独对了苍白的纱窗而沉默
怅望向窗外一点云与一片青天"

珍重竹子

剑龙

1989 年 7 月 29 日

Bamboo:

Read you drunk and greedy laughter, should wake up? Such a big cup to fill, drunken fairy Li Bai is also difficult to do, how willful you are!

My company is carrying out on-the-job training. A lot of review materials are on the table, but I have no intention to study hard. I only to sink into lovesickness.

The wind and rain are drizzling, and the night is empty and. Looking out of the window, who will send the brocade in the clouds? When the wild goose returns, the moon is full of the west building, the silver man is far away, and the stars are shining. Do you know if you are tender, and the good times are like dreams?

The love of Zhimo Xiaoman is beautiful, but the early death of Zhimo makes people sigh. The 50-year life-and-death love of Hugo and Juliet is a thousand-year-old song on earth!

At dusk of slight rain, the breeze is independent, the people who speak slightly speak and the of songs broadcast slightly, to my tipsy drunkenness, whispering under the light, the and gentleness the.

I like a in a pavilion, bird's eye view of the sea, let the eyes of the light man row and row, hear whisper: drunk ah drunk!

Have you read this poem?

"You are the 1 migratory bird that is traveling.

Occasionally

Visited my autumn garden

Without any care, you are far away again.

Far away to the unknowable sky

Are you looking for another garden 1 spring in the?

I am silent to the pale screen alone

Looking out the window, a little cloud and a blue sky"

Take care of bamboo

Jianlong

29 July 1989

竹子：

想你一道小溪汇成一片春潮的情，我知道你此刻，莲花一样的心事。

那曾经拥有过的春光，那曾经拥有过的夏绿，那曾经拥有过的微颤和痴恋，曾经是怎样强烈地拂过我俩的心波？但无论是怎样的努力，也挽不回我决意远去的脚步。

你声声的呼唤在我心底，你心弦弹拨的清音，我虽没和应，唯有化作天边一颗星星，夜夜守在你的窗前。

愿你的心灵永宁。

剑龙又及。

1989 年 7 月 29 日

热爱生命
Love of Life

Bamboo:

　　I miss you when a stream merges into a spring tide. I know your lotus-like thoughts at this moment.

　　How strongly did the spring scenery that we once had, the summer green that we once had, the trembling and infatuation that we once had brushed our hearts? But no matter how hard I tried, I could not pull back the footsteps of my determination to go away.

　　The call of your voice is in my heart, the clear sound of your heartstrings, although I have no response, I can only turn into a star 1 the sky, watching at your window every night.

　　May your heart be forever.

Jianlong
29 July 1989

剑龙：

　　时值深夜两点，窗外大雨倾盆，无眠，起床拧灯，伏案写信给你，恰是夜半无人私语时。

　　不止一次被长辈赞我聪明能干，作为一个女子，谁知我一生不得安宁的，便是这份不可遏制的好强好胜心。

　　我青春的额头虽不曾留下风霜，然而眉宇间，眼眸里，已抹不掉那如雾如烟的沧桑，可慰的是我仍然英年依旧。

　　情之所至，或笑或哭或忧或喜或恼或嗔，信手拈来，皆成文章，但瞬间的思绪，悄然而至，悄然而逝，无影无踪，待成文字，已不及万千，因此，每次读你的信，常有一种情同此心，情出一辙的契合，微笑、微忧，以致捧腹大笑，一切皆成自然。

　　只知道不停地写呀写，写了什么，写了多少，一点都记不起来了。

　　微雨，夜凉，忽记起这首诗：骤雨过后／就像云的出岫／

你一定要原谅／一定要原谅呵／一个女子无端的忧愁。

　　想象自己正是一只在旅行中的候鸟，从这秋的园林，飞到春的园林，世上，云天，再也没有固定的窝。

　　杨贵妃正梨花一枝春带雨地站在我的面前，是梦中或是仙境？我已经不能清醒，想起那首白居易的"长恨歌"，正是"天长地久有时尽，此恨绵绵无绝期"。

祝你

案安。

竹子

1989 年 8 月 10 日

Jianlong:

　　It was two o'clock in the middle of the night, it was raining cats and cats outside the window, and there was no to sleep. I to turn the light I got up and write to you at my desk. It was just the middle of the night when no one was whispering.

　　I have been praised by my elders more than once I am smart and capable. As a woman, who knows that what makes me restless in my life is this unstoppable and competitive heart.

　　Although my youth did not leave wind and frost on my forehead, but between my brow and eyes, can wipe off the vicissitudes of life like fog and smoke. What is comforting is that I am still young.

　　To the love , or laugh or cry or worry or joy or annoyance or angry , come at your fingertips, all become articles, but the thoughts of the moment, quietly come, quietly gone, without a trace, stay there are no more than a thousand words, so every time I read your letter, I often 1 the same feeling, feelings the fit of 1 rut, smile, micro worry , so that laugh, everything is natural.

热爱生命
Love of Life

All I know is that I can't remember what I wrote and how much I wrote.

Light rain, cold night, suddenly remembered this poem: after the shower/ is like a cloud out of the /you must forgive/you must forgive ah /a woman's unprovoked sorrow.

Imagine that you are 1 migratory bird that travels only. From this autumn garden to the spring garden, there is no fixed nest in the world.

Yang Guifei is a pear flower spring with rain standing in front of me, is it a dream or a fairyland? I can no longer wake up, thinking of Bai Juyi's "Eternal Regret Song", which is "everlasting, and this hatred will never end".

Wish you
An case.
Bamboo
August 10, 1989

竹子：

好吗？

刚接兰姐电话，又收到你的信，好开心。

试已考完，七科平均分为 98 分。

我看琼瑶的"十个故事"，那缠绵悱恻的爱情，让人一唱三叹，写爱情是她的拿手好戏，唯是太理想化的人物和情节，削弱了现实的意义。

知识渊博的人，其思绪活跃，其忧也深，人之境界越高往往越孤苦，但追求完美者如夸父追日，永无止息的是对求知的狂与迷。

珍重
剑龙
1989 年 8 月 16 日

Bamboo:

    Okay?

    I just answered Lanjie's phone and received your letter again. I am so happy.

    The test has been completed and the average score of the seven subjects is 98.

    I read Qiong Yao's "Ten Stories", the sentimental love, which makes people sing and sigh, writing love is her specialty, only are too idealized characters and plots, which weaken the meaning of reality.

    People with profound knowledge have active thoughts, and their worries and are also. The higher the realm of people, the more lonely they are. However, those who pursue perfection are like Kuafu chasing the sun. What is never ending is the madness of seeking knowledge and..

Precious
Jianlong
August 16, 1989

剑龙发了这封信后便颇长一段时间都没有再给竹子去信。竹子非常担心,也十分伤感,她写道:

After the sword dragon sent this letter, he did not send any more letters to bamboo for a long time.

    Bamboo was very worried and very sad. She wrote:

剑龙:

    冷血动物,甜心。

    已足足一个月没你的信了,面对收发室伯母无奈的微笑,

热爱生命
Love of Life

我的信心全垮了。

是什么令你硬起心肠？让我饱受这悠悠等待的煎熬？害怕你从此音信全无。

万能的主呵，赐我勇气和信心吧！

竹子
1989年9月1日

Jianlong:

Cold-blooded animals, sweetheart.

I haven't received your letter for a full month, and my confidence has collapsed in the face of aunt's helpless smile in the mail room.

What makes you hard-hearted? Let me suffer from this long waiting torment? I'm afraid you'll never be heard from again.

Almighty Lord, give me courage and confidence!

Bamboo
1 September 1989

竹子：

好吗？

宁愿在暮色之中，轻闭倦眼在椅中，宁愿在灯下翻阅你的心，宁愿一卷诗书在手，椅中枕畔，品味哲理及温情，宁愿一盅清水洒青藤，看欣欣的绿意托着晶莹的水珠，宁愿在沙发上听优柔的柏格尼尼小提琴独奏，或是静听地母的微语，看星光在夜空之中眨眼，四周在夜的统领之下各归其所，各适其适，隐约可闻万物的呼吸，世界很温柔，万物如初生的婴儿沉入梦乡……

我感受到心灵的舒放自由，如花儿夜里静静地开放。

我不思不想，心灵与静夜交流，我接近了自然，我融入了自然，我与天地万物成为一体。

若勤是为了将来的疏狂，我要在此刻饮这杯美酒。

香港著名司仪钟保罗堕楼身亡，因赌而欠下巨债，可叹他在事业如日中天之际撒手尘世，想起他的音容笑貌，知道再坚强的人，人生都会有软弱的时候，不胜唏嘘。

活着是美好的，能体会经历种种人生，战胜种种困难，也是人生的乐趣。

我满怀希望，历我的人生。

珍重竹子

剑龙

1989 年 9 月 4 日

Bamboo:

Okay?

I would rather close my tired eyes in the chair in the twilight, read your heart under the lamp, taste philosophy and warmth 1 a volume of poems and books in my hand, beside the pillow in the of the chair, 1 a cup of clear water sprinkled with green vines, watch Xinxin's green holding crystal-clear water drops, and listen to excellent soft bergonini violin solo on the sofa, or listen and the mother's micro-language, watch the starlight blink in the night sky, all around under the command of the night to its own place, each appropriate, vaguely can hear the breath of all things, the world is very gentle, all things like a newborn baby sank into sleep...

I feel the ease and freedom of my heart, like flowers quietly opening at night.

I don't think about it. My heart communicates with the quiet night. I am close to nature. I am integrated into nature. I am with all things in heaven and earth.

If Qin is for the sake of future dredging, I will drink this cup of wine at this moment.

Hong Kong's famous master of ceremonies, Paul, fell to his death and owed a huge debt due to gambling on. It is a pity that he gave up his life at the height of his career. When he thinks of his voice and smile, he knows that no matter how strong he is, there will be times of weakness in his life.

Living is beautiful, can experience all kinds of life, overcome all kinds of difficulties, is also the joy of life.

I am full of hope and my life.

Take care of bamboo

Jianlong

September 4, 1989

剑龙发出这封信后，收到竹子九月一日的来信，知道她已是情根越种越深，自己也下不了决心，便暂停写信给竹子，希望大家让时间，慢慢将热情冲淡。但他自己也不曾料到，最放不下这份情的原来却是他自己。

十一月初一个傍晚，吃过晚饭，剑龙同老友阿刚如常一起去散步。沿着拱北宾馆的海堤和别墅漫行，剑龙和他相识七年，一中学毕业就考入同一机构工作，经常见面，甘苦与共，一起成长，情如手足。

刚见剑龙有些闷闷不乐，问：

"龙，你有什么心事？"

"我想我爱上了一个女子，可又拿不定主意。"

"原来在走桃花运，她是谁？"

"萧竹子，记得吗我有一张照片，一个女子穿着粉蓝色的长裙在树林中微笑的。"

"记得,她一头瀑布般的秀发很漂亮,身材苗条,长得雅致,你说是你同学。"

"正是。上次回乡时大家久别重逢,发现彼此在爱好情趣上很合拍,舞更是跳得心旌摇荡,她不由自主就堕入情网。"剑龙叹了口气。

"你感觉如何?"阿刚道。

"我觉得大家的交流很有共鸣,问题是她的家人都在香港,她去港定居的行程也近了,她出去是迟早的事,而我的事业在这里,我要选择她,就要放弃现有的事业。"

"这实在是件很为难的事,男人的事业总是最重要的,有事业爱情才可附丽。"

"我也明白这道理,所以我婉拒了她,而且在两个月前狠心不同她通信和电话!可是,我对她的思念却是越来越深,整天想着和她一起度过的快乐时光。"

"可否做一对好朋友?互通音讯应该可以吧?"

"但一通信,她就伤心泪流,弄到我又内疚又心痛!真是进又难退又难。"

"此事关系重大,你若放弃事业,以何为生?她出去后你们的路怎么走?这当中有许多变量和不测,你一定要好好想清楚,一切从长计议。"

……

深秋的时节,小径上飘着落叶,落霞在天边纷飞,秋风带来了寒意,可秋天也是成熟丰收的季节,时光都在岸边延挨着,我要不要将这艘爱船撑了出去?前面是茫茫无涯的未知!

两个月的不通信,剑龙非但没有忘掉竹子,思念反而更

热爱生命 / Love of Life

胜于从前，他于十一月五日的日记之中写了一封信：

After Jianlong sent this letter, she received a letter from bamboo on September 1. Knowing that she was already deeply rooted in and could not make up her mind, she suspended writing to bamboo, hoping that everyone would let time slowly dilute her enthusiasm. However, he himself did not expect that it was himself who could not let go of this feeling.

One evening in early November, after dinner, Jianlong and his old friend Agang went for a walk as usual. Along the seawall and villa of Gongbei Hotel, Jianlong and met him for seven years. After graduating from a middle school, he was admitted to work in the same organization. He often met, shared weal and woe, grew up together, and was like brothers and brothers.

I just saw Jianlong a little unhappy and asked:

"Dragon, what's on your mind?"

"I think I'm in love with a woman, but can't make up his mind ."

"The original is going peach blossom, who is she?"

"Xiao Zhuzi, remember I have a picture of a woman smiling in the woods in a powder blue dress."

"Remember, she has beautiful waterfall hair, slim figure and elegant appearance. You said she was your classmate."

"Exactly. The last time we returned to our hometown, we met again after a long time. We found that we were in tune with each other in terms of hobbies and interests. The dance was and, and she fell in love involuntarily." Jianlong sighed.

"How do you feel?" he said.

"I think everyone's communication is very resonant. The problem is that her family is in Hong Kong, and her journey to settle in Hong Kong is approaching. It is only a matter of time before she goes out. My career is here. If I want to choose her, I have to give up my existing career."

"This is really a very difficult thing. A man's career is always the most important thing. Only with career love can he be attached."

"I also understand this truth, so I declined her, and two months ago, she was cruel to correspondence and phone calls! However, I miss her more and more deeply, thinking about the happy time spent with her all day."

"Could you be a good friend? Should it be possible to exchange audio?"

"But when she 1 the correspondence, she shed tears and made me feel guilty and heartache! It's really difficult to enter and retreat."

"This matter is of great importance. If you give up your career, what is your life? How do you go when she's out? There are many variables and accidents in this. You must think it over and take a long-term view."

...

In late autumn, there are fallen leaves on the path, sunset clouds are flying in the sky, and the autumn wind brings chill., autumn is also the season of mature harvest. Time extends the shore and is close to the. Do I want to this love boat out? Ahead is the boundless unknown!

After two months of non-communication, Jianlong not only did not forget the bamboo, but missed it more than before. He wrote a letter in his diary on November 5:

竹子：

　　好吗？

　　此际，窗外大雨倾盆，哗哗的雨织成了一片漫茫的世界，室外很静，不宁的是我的心绪，昨夜在睡眼蒙眬之中，忧戚睡去，但仍念念不忘的是：已多日没有给你去信和电话。多少次重读你的书简，深深明白你的真情挚意，你的无奈与哀伤。你的心，你为编织情梦时，奏出的美妙乐章，我竟忍心将你一拒再拒！

　　情为何物？事业何价？心灵何价？为何总是度量着种种的得失！

　　苦的是情浓如海。而事业呢？我舍得放弃手中安稳舒适，前途光明的公务员工作？

　　但你那"年初或许要嫁个殷实男子的"的话让我心惊。

　　我不忍你如此一位知情达理，温婉聪慧的女子，委屈于平凡的男子，你心灵中迷人的风姿，你的万种风情，你对文字的热爱，对诗书的钟情痴迷，你宽厚的胸襟，你对爱的理解、投入、勇敢及不求回报的给予，令我赞叹。你我都渴求的，是林间的一个家园，向往的是共同心灵的淡泊宁静。

　　竹子，你是世上，唯一的知我深者。在这个世上，没有谁，如你这般深爱我，理解、欣赏和包容我，让我的生命充实美丽。

　　我俩且哭且笑且歌且舞，生命的源泉得以拓展，一起时，有说不完的话，无论是做任何细小的事情，都快乐愉悦。对书诗的共同痴心，焕发着我俩的精神。

　　细想你学历比我高，家境比我好，前途比我灿烂，但你却选择我，你说只要俩人在一起，你甘愿过清贫日子，品格是多么高尚。

但我亦清楚，若选择你，我的生活将是漂泊无定，以及无尽的等待，也不知安宁若我，可承受得了，这不定岁月的摧磨？

一个是情场痴子，一个是恋海冤家，若是没奇缘，偏偏今生遇着你。

梧桐树，三更雨，不道离情正苦，一叶叶，一声声，空阶滴到明。

我若将你放弃，也许会抱憾终身。真是进退两难，费尽思量！

剑龙
1989年11月5日

Bamboo:

Okay?

At this time, the rain poured out of the window, and the rattling rain weaved into a and world. The outside was very quiet. What was restless was my mood. Last night, I was asleep with my eyes and. I fell asleep with sadness, but what I still remember is: I haven't sent you a letter or phone call for many days. How many times to reread your book, deeply understand your sincere intention, your helpless and sad. Your heart, the wonderful music you played when you to weave your dream, I have the heart to 1 you and refuse you again!

What is love? What is the price of career? What is the price of heart? Why do you always measure all kinds of gains and losses!

The bitter is as thick as the sea. and career? Am I willing to give up a job as a civil servant that is secure and comfortable in my hands and has a bright future?

But your words "maybe you'll marry a rich man at the beginning

热爱生命
Love of Life

of the year" make me scared.

I cannot bear that you are so 1 a sensible, gentle and intelligent woman, wronged by ordinary men, your charming charm in your heart, your love for words, your love for poems and books, your and generous mind, your understanding of love, devotion, brave and unrequited giving, which make me admire. What you and I both desire is a home in the forest, and what we yearn for is the tranquility of the common mind.

Bamboo, you are the only one in the world who knows my depth. In this world, there is no one who loves me as much as you do, understands, appreciates and embraces me, and makes my life full and beautiful.

We cried and laughed and and sang and danced. The source of life was expanded. When we were together, we had endless words to say. No matter what we did, we were happy and joyful. The common infatuation for books and poems coruscates our spirits.

I think you have a higher education background than me, a better family background than me, and a brighter future than me, but you chose me. You said that as long as the two are together, you are willing to live in poverty and how noble your character is.

But I also know that if I choose you, my life will be wandering and endless waiting, and I don't know peace. If I can bear it, will be destroyed by the of uncertain years?

One is a love affair, the other is a friend who loves the sea. If there is no strange fate, it happened that I met you in this life.

The buttonwood tree, the third more rain, does not leave feeling is bitter, a leaf, a sound, empty step drops to Ming.

If I give you up, I may regret it for life. What a dilemma!

Jianlong
November 5, 1989

剑龙虽然没有将此信寄出,但仿佛灵机一动,深情已如离弦的箭,向着爱情直射过去,生命诚可贵,爱情价更高,剑龙已经不由自主地,执迷于爱情,心甘情愿焚身以火。由11月6日开始,思念使剑龙如痴如狂,他冲破了所有思想的阻力,决意去赴,这不能饮不可饮,亦要拼却的一场爱的酒醉!

Although Jianlong did not send this letter, it seemed that had a brainwave. Deep feeling was like an arrow from the string, shooting directly at love. Life was precious and love was more expensive. Jianlong was already involuntarily obsessed with love and was willing to burn himself to fire. Starting from November 6, missing made Jianlong crazy. He broke through all the resistance of his thoughts and decided to go. This is not to drink, he to fight but 1 a love drunkenness!

竹子:

我爱。

离别了两个多月,我以为我已忘却,谁知思念更甚,忆我俩相知的情意,念你的伤心苦痛,我的泪在心内渗,正是:

新来瘦,非干病酒,不是悲秋。

腕底的笔这般沉重,一如我的心,我孜孜不倦地沉浸于文学的艺术之中,没有你的欣赏和共鸣,何来喜悦?知音世所稀,人生永恒是不泯的记忆,岁月流不走真爱,如果我俩是如此的倾慕和依恋,又岂可轻言离别?

剪不断,理还乱,是离愁,别有一番滋味在心头。

苦了你呵，我的竹子。

多情自古伤离别，更那堪冷落清秋节，整整七年鱼雁传情，故旧岂能忘怀，而不令人追忆？相识天下，唯你相知。

爱你的心灵和品格，我缤纷的情意和风采要向你展示，让你彻底读懂我的灵魂之语。

不止一次欲执笔续我俩之缘，草好的信积在抽屉，言语难以诉说心事于万一。在忧思之中时光飞逝，又时光难挨，两个多月就这般过去了，而我是如此珍惜我俩的情缘。

雨后，凉云住了，阳光洒进了暖意，鲜芳的空气中，似又再有悦耳的仙乐响起，仿佛听到百鸟在林中歌唱，连路边的车辆也富于喜气的动感节奏，我感觉到一种愉悦的新意，环绕着我，我明白到自己追求的，是你美好的品格和心灵，是一段美好的爱恋。

庆幸我俩的理智和情感同样丰厚。

爱的微妙，在于相互的接纳，包容，外人的判定评价又算得了什么？

正是：山重水复疑无路，柳暗花明又一村。可爱的竹子，你是否也感到，有一阵惊喜自天边破云而来？——那就是我的觉醒。

伸出你的手，让我俩紧紧相握，来创一段美丽的爱恋，若爱之途有百花盛开，我俩要共同呼吸、陶醉；若上苍用困苦考验，让我俩一起承受；爱一定会给予我俩勇气和信心，相信我俩的才智，相信我俩融合的力量，抬起头来呵竹子，天边已为我俩显露了希望的曙光。

纸短情长，让我俩凝眸相握，紧紧拥抱！

想念你的

剑龙

1989年11月6日

Bamboo:

My love.

Two months I left, I thought I had forgotten, but I missed it even more. I remember the affection we knew each other, read your sadness and pain, and my tears seep in my heart. It is:

The new lean, non-dry sick wine, not sad autumn.

The pen at the bottom of my wrist is so heavy, just like my heart, I am tirelessly immersed in the art of literature. Without your appreciation and resonance, how can I be happy? The bosom friend is rare in the world, life is eternal memory, and years cannot flow away from true love. If we are so admired and attached, how can we say goodbye lightly?

Cut constantly, reason also disorderly, is the sorrow of parting, don't have a taste in my heart.

Bitter you, my bamboo.

Affection has been parting since ancient times, and it is even more deserving of the Qingqiu Festival. For seven years, fish and geese have been spreading their feelings. How can the old days be forgotten and not recalled? Know the world, only you know.

Love your heart and character, I colorful affection and elegant demeanor to show you, so that you thoroughly and read the words of my soul.

More than once I wanted to write to continue our relationship, I wrote good letters in the drawer, and it was difficult for words to tell what was on my mind in case. In the midst of worry, time flies, and time is difficult to, more than two months passed like this, and I so to cherish our love.

热爱生命
Love of Life

After the rain, the cool clouds, the sun shone into the warm, the fresh fragrant air, the like and the melodious fairy music sounded again, as if to hear birds singing in the forest, even the roadside vehicles are full of happy dynamic rhythm, I feel 1 is a kind of happy new idea, around me, I understand that is what I to pursue, is your good character and heart, is a good love.

I am glad that we are equally rich in reason and emotion.

The subtlety of love lies in mutual acceptance and tolerance. What is the judgment and evaluation of outsiders?

Exactly: there is no way out, and there is another village. Lovely bamboo, do you also feel that a surprise has come from sky breaking through the clouds?–That is my awakening.

Stretch out your hand and let us hold each other tightly to a beautiful love. if there are flowers in full bloom on the way to love, we should breathe and be intoxicated together. If God use hardships and tests to let us bear them together. Love will definitely give us courage and confidence, believe in our intelligence, believe in the power of our integration, raise our heads and bamboo, the horizon has revealed a glimmer of hope for both of us.

Paper is short and love is long, let us hold and hug each other tightly!

miss you
Jianlong
November 6, 1989

竹子：

我爱。

让我爱你只为你可爱，让我爱你，因你的品格高尚，让

剑龙与竹子的情书,惊艳了岁月
Jianlong and bamboo love letter, amazing years

我爱你,因我时刻想你念你,因为你已经深深地占满了我的心。

从来没有如此刻这般热烈、深刻地渴见你,爱你胜于从前。

若我曾无情伤害过你,允许我以衷情爱恋,轻柔地抚慰你,你可明白,我此际的心情此刻的真?可知我笔下不曾放弃的挣扎?

愿我的爱,驱散你心头的荫云,莫道轻荫便拟归。知否爱的园林,还有满眼的森林、绿草,有繁花似锦?让我俩的风采和情韵,在彼此的跟前,如花瓣一样,一片片舒展开来;任我俩在当中,尽情地呼吸沉醉,身心在领略交流之中,满足畅快。

我俩是一双美丽的鸟儿,要比翼齐飞,放声鸟啭呵,在这美妙的爱的园林。

竹子,请握起你的笔,用心灵以不羁,倾诉你的衷心,爱的热情太脆弱,有时会很容易被扼杀,但曾经沧海,让我俩学会珍惜。来来来,请用爱在我俩心间植一把爱苗,在春暖花开的季节,长成一丛丛肆意生长的绚烂姿容。

爱给了我热情和自由,我的一支笔就谱成了舒畅的行云流水,让情韵合于自然,随心所欲,由笔端漫卷而去。

我感到幸福、兴奋和神采飞扬,心灵颤抖,呵呵,我沉寂多时的爱的岩浆,顷刻间复活喷涌而出,我如何抑制得了,这汹涌的情潮?我此际的思绪明澈,万千的思绪在我希望和记忆之中穿行,我心怀散射阳光,百卉和绿意溢满心间,情感之林已百木茂盛,欣欣的生机,是严冬之后大地的复苏。

或许世上还有不少女子比你娇艳,但你的品格更胜一筹,爱一经选择,则有一份责任感伴随于心,世间再多的女子已是无缘。

请相信情的坚贞,相信我不会是风流成性的男子,我相

热爱生命
Love of Life

信灵与肉的结合，才是最美妙的享受。

前路，不管如何，我愿给你一副共担风雨的肩，让你疲倦时拥你入怀，让你在人海之中，不再落寞，不再孤独，不再惊惶。

原来上苍对一切早有安排，一切都是为了我俩握手同行的今朝。

你我的生命，因有爱而充满奋斗创拓的豪情和力量。

不再拒绝承认这份深爱，只愿在往后的日子里，寄给你多几许欢欣，多几许快慰。

大雨过后，就如云的出岫，不绝如缕的烟云，是我俩缠绵的情怀，我爱三毛、琼瑶、冰心、泰戈尔、席慕蓉这些厚爱的灵魂，爱一切善良而至情至圣的人类。

今年，我参加了机关的征文比赛，我的作品《不亦快哉》荣获冠军。在此，也请你来分享我的喜悦。

今夜月白风清，我的心也因向你倾诉而充满快慰和喜悦。

思念很美，交流很美，我又再回复到往日挥写自由的境界，有不竭的文思由心间热烈地涌起……

竹子为我珍重。

剑龙

1989 年 11 月 7 日

Bamboo:

I love.

Let me love you only for your lovely, let me love you, because of your noble character, let me love you, because I miss you all the time, because you have filled my heart deeply.

Never before have I been so eager and deeply to see you and love you more than ever before.

If I have hurt you mercilessly and allowed me to gently comfort you with affection and love, do you understand the truth of my mood at this moment? Do you know the struggle I never gave up?

May my love scatter the shade of your heart and, and light shade shall be. Do you know the garden of love, as well as the forest, green grass and flowers? Let our elegant demeanour and charm, in front of each other, like petals, stretch out one by one; Let us breathe heartily in the middle, and let our body and mind enjoy the exchange, and be satisfied and carefree.

We are 1 pair of beautiful birds, to fly together with wings, and the singing birds trill, in this wonderful garden of love.

Bamboo, please hold your pen and pour out your heart with unruly heart. The passion of love is too fragile and sometimes it is easy to be strangled. but has been through the sea, so we can learn to cherish it. Come on, please use love to plant a of love seedlings between our hearts. In the warm spring season, they grow into clusters of gorgeous looks that grow wantonly.

Love has given me enthusiasm and freedom, and my pen has become a comfortable flowing water, making love and rhyme fit in with nature, free to do what you want, and from the pen end to roll away.

I feel happy, excited and in high spirits, and my heart trembles. Ha ha, the lava of my love, which has been silent for a long time, is resurrected and spewed out in an instant. How can I restrain it, the surging tide of love? My thoughts at this time are clear. Thousands of thoughts are walking through my hopes and memories. My heart is scattering sunshine. Hundreds of flowers and greenery fill my heart.

热爱生命
Love of Life

The forest of emotion is already flourishing trees. The vitality of Xinxin is the recovery of the earth after the severe winter.

Perhaps there are many women in the world who are more delicate and charming than you, but your character is better. once you love, there is a sense of responsibility in your heart. no matter how many women in the world are, there is no chance.

Please believe in the firmness of love, believe that I will not be a romantic man, I believe that the combination of spirit and flesh is the most wonderful enjoyment.

In the future, no matter what, I would like to give you 1 shoulder to share the wind and rain, let you hold you in your arms when you are tired, and let you be in the sea of people, no longer lonely, no longer scared.

It turns out that God has already arranged for everything. Everything is for the present when we shake hands with each other.

Your life and mine are full of pride and strength to struggle create because of love and.

No longer refuse to admit this deep love, I only wish to send you more joy and more in the days to come.

After the heavy rain, it was like a cloud of, and the endless clouds of smoke were our lingering feelings. I love the souls of San Mao, Qiong Yao, Bing Xin, Tagore and Xi Murong, and all the kind and most holy human beings.

This year, I took part in the essay competition of the government, and my work "not as fast as possible" won the championship. I invite you to share my joy.

Tonight the moon is white and the wind is clear, and my heart is filled with joy and joy because I confide in you.

Missing is very beautiful, communication is very beautiful, I have returned to the former state of writing freely, there are inexhaustible literary thoughts surging from hearts...

Bamboo for me treasure.

Jianlong
7 November 1989

竹子：

好吗？

知否我在想念你？想起你的孤寂，我心痛。醉过知酒浓，爱过知情重，记否"蕾"：

一个年轻的笑

一股蕴藏的爱

一坛原封的酒

一个未完成的理想

一颗正待燃烧的心

我的激情在涌动，我生活的能量待发放。

竹子，容我爱你，容我爱你的全部。容我奉上一份真诚与执着，让我俩合奏一曲深情的爱情乐章，合写美丽的爱情诗篇。

秋瑟冬寒之后，总有春暖夏艳，走过沙漠，才知道泉水的可贵，两颗历过沧桑的心，有缘在此相会，世上还有什么比这更珍贵？

一只雪般的鸥鸟，悄然仙临我俩面前，这悄然而至的幸福与和平，带着堪怜的怯意，怕被惊起，所以请你也着意地珍惜。

笑容融化于夕阳里，多少往事，都付与晚霞夕照。

众里寻他千百度，蓦然回首，那人却在灯火阑珊处。

守得云开见月明，秋夜之笛音已无哀怨，而绕着甜柔蜜

热爱生命
Love of Life

糖一般的芳香,天庭辽阔,万籁俱寂,希望充满四周,幸福在我青春的面上舒放光彩,镀上洒脱俊逸的气质,身心如草木逢春,又现生机,活力四溅。

愿这活力也注入你的体内,让那沉睡的感情再次熊熊燃烧起来,这正如我写给你的诗:爱你 / 就让爱火 / 热烈地燃烧 / 即便成灰 / 亦因曾经深爱过 / 而无悔地 / 荡飘!

入夜,你的芳息,如一簇静静的幽兰在我的周遭散发;你的倩影,则是摇曳于风中那株垂柳;你是星光下的含笑,是微雨中的丁香,是初春时节的水仙。竹子我爱,请凝望着我,自信你眸子的晶亮;请让你神采飞扬的脸庞光芒四射,恋爱中的女人有着无比的妩媚,也请你,欢跃你白杨般轻盈的腰身,为我俩欢笑,为生命的美丽讴歌,对花儿问好,给草儿亲吻,想念我时,尽情地在腕底倾诉。

无论你成功或失败,欢乐与痛苦,我要永为你深情的关注,容我分享你的快乐,也容我分担你的忧惧。

野火烧不尽,春风吹又生,陶庐的隐逸,淡泊的情怀,在我的灵府深处。容我俩拥抱相爱!

依依道珍重。

剑龙

1989年11月8日

Bamboo:

    Okay?

    Do you know I'm missing you? Think of your loneliness, I heartache. Drunk know wine strong, love know heavy, remember "Lei":

    A young laugh

    1 shares of love

    1 jar of wine intact

An unfinished ideal

1 a heart to burn

My passion is surging, and the energy of my life is to be released.

Bamboo, let I love you, let all I love you. Let me present a sincere and persistent, let us play a deep love movement together, write a beautiful love poem.

After autumn and winter are cold, there is always warm spring and beautiful summer. Only when you walk through the desert can you know the value of spring water. Two hearts that have experienced vicissitudes of life in the are destined to meet here. What is more precious than this in the world?

1 a snow-like gull bird, quietly the fairy in front of us, this quietly arrived happiness and peace, with pitiful timidity, afraid of being alarmed, so please cherish it intentionally.

Smile melts in the sunset, how many past events, all to pay the sunset.

The crowd looked for him thousands of times, suddenly looking back, but the man was in the dim light.

Watched the clouds open to see the moon, the autumn night flute sound has no sorrow, and the around the sweet soft honey-like fragrance, the vast heaven, the is silent and, hope is full of all around, happiness in my youth face relaxed and glorious, plated with free and easy and handsome temperament, body and mind like vegetation in spring, and now vitality, vitality splash everywhere.

May this vitality also be injected into your body, and let the sleeping feelings burn brightly again. This is just like the poem I wrote to you: love you/let love the fire /burn enthusiastically/even if it becomes ashes/

热爱生命
Love of Life

because I once loved deeply/without regret/ to float!

At night, your fragrance is, like a cluster of and quiet orchid spreading around me. Your beautiful image is the weeping willow swaying in the wind. You are a smile under the starlight, a clove in the light rain, and a daffodil in early spring. Bamboo I love, please gazing at me, confident of your eyes bright; please let your radiant face shine brightly, the woman in love has a very charming, also please, joy you poplar like light waist, for us to laugh, for the beauty of life, to say hello to the flowers, give grass kiss, miss me, heartily in wrist bottom talk.

Whether you succeed or fail, joy or pain, I will always be your affectionate attention, allow me to share your joy, and allow me to share your fears.

Wildfire burns endlessly, spring breeze blows again, Tao Lu's seclusion and indifferent feelings are in the depths of my spiritual mansion. Let us embrace love!

Yiyidao treasure.

Jianlong

8 November 1989

竹子：

我爱。

由心底呼唤你，依依切切，你可曾听见？

泰戈尔写过：

"假如我今生无缘遇见你，就让我永远感到恨不相逢——让我念念不忘，让我在醒时梦中都怀带着这悲哀的苦痛。

当我的日子在世界的闹市中度过，我的双手满捧着每日赢利的时候，让我觉得我一无所获——让我念念不忘，让我在醒时梦中都怀带着这悲哀的苦痛。

……"

容我向你诉说我的衷心。

我选择了你,因我需要你,因我只需要你,我俩的情意已痴缠一起,仿佛春蚕吐丝,至死方休。

当日寻寻觅觅,冷冷清清,今日是春光烂漫,处处生机,憬将来,良辰美景,赏心乐事,都由我俩双手创拓。

我俩有聪明才智,有投契的心性,我俩年轻,有无限的潜力,爱中投入全副身心,才不辜负韶华情缘。

让我俩容纳彼此的全部,继而改善,无论生活如何变迁,也始终携手同行,始终崇尚智慧,执着于真、善、美。

闻一多先生写道:

生命是一张没价值的白纸

自从绿给了我发展

红给了我热情

黄教我以忠义

蓝教我以高洁

粉红赐我以希望

灰白赠我以悲哀

再完成这张彩图

黑还要加我以死亡

从此以后

我便溺爱于我的生命

因为我爱它的色彩

是的,生命的五彩缤纷,我俩应当心存感激,学习热爱生命。

生命之路上,快乐的足印好轻快,唯独忧伤凄楚,共同

热爱生命
Love of Life

的苦难才永远的镂人心坎，苦难的历练，会给我们以成熟沉稳的报酬。

落花人独立，微雨燕双飞，在你离别故乡的日子里，我只有长久地将你思念，长久地将你等待，以我男子汉的忠诚，笑容里为你祝福。

金风玉露一相逢，便胜却人间无数！离别，若是两情久长时，又岂在朝朝暮暮？只是我恨不能给你富足的生活，担心你跟我受苦，担心你的父母不支持你投入一个清贫男子的怀抱。

我担心，若放弃现有的事业，何以为生？但若前思后想，心中的怯弱便会阻止了脚步，还是让我鼓起勇气吧。

竹子，你是涓滴的清泉，纯洁、痴绝、甘润，你的爱傲雪不屈，坚韧不拔，是我甜睡时的温柔，是我焦渴时的甘霖。让我爱你青春欢唱的时辰，也爱你为爱而添的风霜。

你家中的琐事可解决了？许多事，有时间与智慧，假以时日，都会一一得到解决，我们只有凡事尽力而为，而已。

拥抱你！

剑龙

1989年11月9日

Bamboo:

My love.

Calling you from the bottom of my heart, yiyi earnestly, have you ever heard?

Tagore wrote:

"If I have no chance to meet you in this life, let me always feel hate not to meet–let me never forget, let me wake up with this sad pain in my dream.

When I spend my days in the downtown of the world, and my

hands are full of daily profit, let me feel that I have gained nothing–let me never forget, let me wake up with this sad pain in my dreams.

..."

Let me tell you my heart.

I chose you, because I need you, because I only need you, our feelings have tangled together, like spring silkworms spinning silk until death.

The day of searching, desolation, today is the spring, everywhere vitality, the future of the, beautiful scenery, pleasure, by me and hands create.

We are intelligent and congenial. We are young and have unlimited potential. Only by devoting ourselves to love can we live up to Yunhua's love.

Let us accommodate all of each other and then improve. No matter how our lives change, we will always walk hand in hand, always and advocate and wisdom, and persist in truth, goodness and beauty.

Mr. Wen Yiduo wrote:

Life is a worthless piece of white paper.

Since the green gave me development

Red gave me enthusiasm.

Huang taught me loyalty

Blue taught me to be noble

Pink gives me hope

Gray give me to sorrow

Complete this color chart again.

Black will add me to death.

Since then

Love of Life

I will spoil my life

Because I love its color

Yes, life is colorful. We should be grateful and learn to love life.

On the road of life, the footprints of happiness are light and fast, but sadness and sadness are the only way to the human heart forever. The experience of suffering will give us a mature and steady reward.

Falling flowers are independent and swifts fly in pairs. In the days when you leave your hometown, I can only miss you for a long time and wait for you for a long time. With my manly loyal, I will bless you in my smile.

Gold wind jade dew 1 meet, then win the world countless! Departing, if the two love for a long time, is it in the twilight? It's just that I wish I could give you a rich life, worry about your suffering with me, and worry that your parents don't support you into the arms of a poor man.

I worry that if you give up your existing career, how can you live? But if you think about it, the weakness in your heart will stop you from walking. Let me summon up courage.

Bamboo, you are a trickle of clear spring, pure, delusive and sweet. Your love is unyielding and indomitable. It is the gentleness of my sweet sleep and the showers of my thirst. Let me love the hours of your youth and the of your love.

Can you solve the chores in your family? Many things, with time and wisdom, will be solved one by one in time. We can only do our best in everything.

Embrace you!
Jianlong
9 November 1989

竹子：

在灯下痴痴地想念着你

静夜中倚枕沉思，萦回的是脉脉温情，悠悠白云我意，明月千里我心。

你离开之后，星不再亮，月失去光芒，天不会蓝，鸟儿也沉默了歌声。

智利诗人斯密特拉尔的《我喜欢爱情》：

它在田野上自由漫步，它在清风中展动翅膀

它在丽日下纵情欢跳，它把松林点缀得辉煌

你真不该将它遗忘，像扔掉一种坏的思想，它在机智的反驳中握有敏锐的道理

它有学者的论据，但使用的是女人的柔腔

你真该有人的理智，而不是玄妙的思想，你必须坚信爱力量

它给你缠上亚麻绷带，你必须忍受创伤

它献给你温馨的臂膀，你不知它遁向何方

它走了，你神魂颠惚地尾随，尽管你发现：你必须追随它，直到死亡

我爱月在松间照的空灵，我爱归隐田园的隐逸，我可适于万丈红尘之中，也可满足于清贫的生活，我知足，我随遇而安而又保有奋斗的意志，我有游戏人生的态度。

我愿给你我永恒的忠心、诚意和共同开拓生活的双手和才智。

智利另一位诗人维多夫罗的《咱们俩》：

咱们俩就像是

同一条河里的两道涟漪

咱们俩就像是

热爱生命
Love of Life

同一朵花里的两颗露滴

咱们是一颗星里的两道光辉

一把琵琶弹出的两个音符

咱们是一个窝中的两只小鸟

是共同爱情的两滴泪珠

这恰恰说出了我俩的心声!

我的心事如星如雨,执笔时,文思泉涌,倾泻而下,绵绵无绝。

何当共剪西窗烛,再话巴山夜雨时,思君时,一派豪情,寸心万里,纷飞的思绪,一任南飞又北飞!

离情正引千丝乱,但兴奋的心情,见证着我又一个不眠的夜晚。

由11月6日至今,我不停地写,但寄去的文字仍未见回音,心中不知你的想法如何?不会让我突然而来的激情吓着了?

满目青山楼外楼,离人更在青山外,罢罢!

用我的臂弯将你拥紧。

剑龙

1989年11月10日

Bamboo:

  Under the lamp thinking of you

  In the quiet night, leaning on the pillow and meditating, what lingers is the warmth of the pulse, the long white clouds and the bright moon.

  After you leave, the star no longer bright, month lose its light, the sky will not be blue, and the birds will be silent singing.

  Chilean poet Smitral's "I like love":

It walks freely in the fields, it spreads its wings in the breeze

It danced with joy in the beautiful sun, and it decorated the pine forest with splendor.

You really shouldn't forget it, 1 a bad thought like throwing away, it holds a sharp point in a witty retort.

It has a scholar's argument, but it uses the soft cavity of a woman.

You really should have human reason, not mysterious thoughts. You must believe in the power of love.

It puts a linen bandage on you and you have to endure the trauma

It's dedicated to your warm arms, you don't know where it to escape

It's gone, you to follow it a trance–like, even though you find that you must follow it until you die.

I love the ethereal spirit of the in the pine space for months. I love the seclusion of returning to the countryside. I can be suitable for the world of mortals, or I can be satisfied with the poor life. I am satisfied. I am content with the situation and keep the will to struggle. I have the attitude of playing life.

I would like to give you my eternal loyalty, sincerity and the hands and wisdom to open up life together.

1 is another poet of Chile, "We Two":

It's like we're both

Two ripples in the same river

It's like we're both

Two drops of dew in the same flower

We are two lights in the 1 star

A lute pops two notes

Love of Life

We are two birds in a nest

Is the common love of two drops of tears

That speaks to both of us!

My mind is like a star, like rain, when writing, literary thought springs, pouring down, endless.

When cutting candles in the west window, and then the words Bashan night rain, think of your, a school of lofty sentiments, inch heart thousands of miles, swirling thoughts, a fly south and to the north to!

The departure is leading thousands of silk disorderly, but the excited mood, witnessed me another sleepless night.

Since November 6, I have been writing, but the text sent by the has not been answered. I don't know what you think in my heart? Won't I be frightened by my sudden passion?

There are many green hills outside the building, and people are even more outside the green hills. Let's go!

Hold you my arms tight.
Jianlong
November 10, 1989

竹子：

可好？

想你在灯下，想你此刻也如我想你这般想念我。

之前看了几个小时的书，席慕蓉在《悲喜剧》中写道：

才发现原来所有的昨日

都是一种不可少的安排

都只是为了好在此刻

让我温柔怜惜地拥你入怀

……

当千帆过尽你翩然来临

我将藏起所有的酸辛

……

我的竹子呵,你正是这千帆过尽之后,那翩临于我的生活的女子,在流下悔泪前,与我紧紧地相拥。

爱是生命的源泉,两颗成熟的心结合在一起,就会碰撞出耀眼的火花。丝丝真情,由心间弹起,荡开去,微颤,悠扬,袅袅不绝如缕……

我倦了,伴我入梦吧,亲爱的竹子。

剑龙
1989 年 11 月 11 日

Bamboo:

Okay?

I miss you under the lamp, and I miss you as much as I miss you at the moment.

After reading the book for several hours before, Xi Murong wrote in "tragicomedy:

Only to find the original all yesterday

1 is an indispensable arrangement.

All just for good at the moment

Let me hold you tenderly and pity

...

When Qian Fan is over, your is coming.

I will hide all the sour

...

My bamboo, you it was after the end of this thousand sails that the woman who in my life hugged me tightly before she shed tears of regret.

Love is the source of life. When two mature hearts are combined, they will collide with dazzling sparks. The real feelings, from the heart bounce, swing away, tremble, melodious, curl curl wisps...

I am tired, accompany me to dream, dear bamboo.

Jianlong
November 11, 1989

竹子：

窗外正阳光灿烂，晴空万里。

曹雪芹说："世事洞明皆学问，人情练达即文章。"

想你也该收到我的信了，每日一封切切的呼唤，你可明白我的心声？

电影"故乡行"的老奶奶就是因错过了好姻缘，一生都在单相思之中度过，多遗憾！

泰戈尔的《流萤集》：

让我们的爱情

像阳光一样包围着你

而又给你光辉灿烂的自由

纪伯伦的《婚姻》：

你们生即同在你们也将永远同在

……

但是在你们契合中保留些空隙吧

让天堂之风在你们之间舞蹈

彼此相爱却又不要使爱成为枷锁

不如让它像在你俩灵魂之岸间流动的海水

……

正如琵琶的各弦线是分开的虽然它们在同一乐曲下颤动

……

站立在一起但不要彼此太靠近

因为庙宇的柱子分开矗立

橡树和绿杉也不能在彼此的阴影中生长

看文学大师对爱和婚姻的描述，如春风拂面，散我疑惑，爱中既占有又有自由，给予又获取，事物总是有矛盾的统一体，生死、苦乐、得失，好坏都在其中了，你说对不对？

自我作出抉择，我的心情畅快，身飘飘如仙，想象你在跟前与我对话，笔在纸上沙沙欢跳，将我一颗爱情之心写满信笺。

有多少话要向你细诉？有多少事要待商讨？

你是我绝佳的舞伴，我俩以情韵，以灵魂来舞蹈，踏着如水的步子，在平滑的云石光波中穿行，我俩也相依相偎，以曼妙的微步，如微启的莲花，散放情人温馨的幽香。

何时你我再一同起舞？

纸在笔下沙沙，我默默地用这笔编织我俩的爱情，只望织出一张锦绣的图画。我是一只在不停地吐着情丝的蚕，好像要至死方休。

我想在亭中眺望故乡，我想把握住点点流光。

相思本是无凭语，还向花笺费泪行，从别后，忆相逢，几回梦魂与君同？

想摘一朵素花，放在碧油油的水面，流去呵，流去，流到我爱人的廊前……

若你见到那花开在你的裙边，请将它缀于你的胸前，让我可时时呼吸到你的体香……

容我吻在你的唇上，吻落你的发香。

剑龙
1989 年 11 月 12 日

Bamboo:

The sun is shining and the sky is clear outside the window.

Cao Xueqin said, "The world is full of knowledge, and human feelings are full of articles."

I think it's time for you to receive my letter, a daily and heartfelt call. Do you understand my heart?

The grandmother in the movie "Hometown Tour" missed a good marriage and spent her life in unrequited love. What a pity!

tagore's "firefly collection"

Let our love

Surrounding you like the sun

And give you glorious freedom

Gibran's Marriage:

You were born be with you and you will always be with you.

...

But leave some space in your fit.

Let the wind of heaven dance between you

Love each other but don't make love a chain

Why don't you make it like water flowing between the on the shore of your souls?

...

Just as the strings of the lute are separate, though they tremble under the same piece of music.

...

Stand together but not too close to each other

For the pillars of the temple stand apart

Oak and green fir can't grow in each other's shadow

Looking at the description of love and marriage by literary masters, such as the spring breeze blowing on the face, the is scattered I wonder, love has both possession and freedom, giving and acquisition, things always have a contradictory unity, life and death, bitterness, gain and loss, good and bad are all in it, are you right?

When I make a choice, I feel carefree and fluttering like a fairy. I imagine you talking to me in front of me, the pen rustling on the paper, writing me 1 a heart of love all over the letterhead.

How many things do I have to tell you about? How many things are to be discussed?

You are my perfect partner for dancing. We dance with emotion and soul. We walk through the smooth clouds and light waves with steps like water. We also snuggle up to each other. with and graceful steps, we like lotus flowers in, spreading the warm and fragrance of lover's.

When will you and I dance together again?

Paper in the pen, I silently use this to weave our love, only hope to weave a picture of splendid. I am the 1 silkworm that is constantly spitting love threads. It seems to be to death.

I want to overlook my hometown in the pavilion, and I want to grasp a little bit of streamer.

Acacia is a language without basis, but also to spend tears line, from goodbye, remember to meet, how many times dream soul with you?

I want to pick a green flower, put it on the water of green oil, flow away, flow away, flow to my lover's gallery ...

If you see the flower blooming on your skirt, please it on your chest so that I can breathe your fragrance from time to time...

Let me kiss on your lips, kiss off the fragrance of your hair.

Jianlong

November 12, 1989

竹子：

好吗？

没有生命的泪与笑，我们不会懂得珍惜，我知道我想要成为你心中，最柔软那个角落的领主，那个地方含泪，也带有丁香一样结着的愁怨。

生命原是一个不断受伤和不断地复原的过程，世界仍然是一个在温柔地等待成熟的果园，天好蓝，树正绿，生活原是可以，如此的宁静和美丽。

每天给你一封信，只愿你珍惜我对你的一片情深。

甜甜地睡去吧，梦中伴我入梦，伴我思念。

我想了两个笔名：飘鹤与潇竹，喜不喜欢？

剑龙

1989 年 11 月 13 日

Bamboo:

Okay?

Without tears and smiles of life, we will not know how to cherish them. I know that I want to be the Lord in the softest corner of your heart. There are tears in that place, and there is also a sorrow like lilac.

Life was originally a process of constant injury and constant recovery. The world is still an orchard gently waiting for maturity. The sky is blue and the trees are green. Life was originally possible, so quiet and beautiful.

I give you a letter every day, only wish you cherish my deep love for you.

Go to sleep sweetly, dream with my dream, with my thoughts.

I think of two pseudonyxs: Floating Crane and Xiao Zhu, do you like it?

Jianlong

November 13, 1989

竹子:

都好吧?

梦中醒时都是你,你是我无处不在的神灵。

相思已经渗入心肺,浓烈、亢奋、激动、颤抖,如惊涛拍岸,不可息止,心里梦里都饱蕴相思。

仍未收到你的回信,信件来回的时间太慢,等待的时光悠长而熬人,看书倦了,抬头时,你的凝望在那蝴蝶兰的绿叶之中。洒水给绿叶,念你舍内的青枝,两情相悦,也不过如此吧。

闻天宇奏着我俩相爱的乐章,和谐之乐由夜莺唱起,安琪儿扑翅在月下飞翔,银辉泻地,泻在沉入梦乡的山百合,月染山更幽,万物都沉醉在满足的静默之中。我想你暂时的沉寂,为的是日后狂泻而下的积蓄,什么都要放出呵,堕入情网的爱侣!

我俩就要起航,天边飘着美好的云朵,海天任我俩翱翔,我俩如一支离弦的箭,将希望射向远方,快乐如飞溅的珠玉,如喷发的焰火亮在夜空。

让我俩执着,人生之途免不了悲喜,免不了考验,但若我俩相爱,一定可战胜困顿;让我俩一道春风得意,也一道落难萧条;让你的柔情拂去我的劳尘,也让我的关切,理你发端的忧伤,让我俩倦时,也紧紧地拥抱在一起。让我俩紧紧相握,相依为命,让你成为我的贤妻,孩子的慈母,我俩共同朋友的良伴。

　　我在藤椅上写信给你，笔端萦绕着对你深深的甜蜜的爱意。

　　今夜月华如练，我俩韶华正当年，沐浴在爱的海洋之中。

　　这叶落的深秋，落叶舞出了我俩一叶叶爱情的故事，舞出了属于我俩成熟的季节。

　　想象你灯下读着我的信，读着我俩共同喜爱的诗篇，或是在夜半无人私语时，给我写信，心中感到无比的幸福。

　　我愿以我毕生的爱，来疼你、宠你，让你自由舒放，长成那恣意生长的山百合。

　　若有山花插满头，我在丛中笑。

　　容我温柔地，怜惜地拥你入怀……

你的飘鹤，
剑龙
1989 年 11 月 14 日

Bamboo:

　　All right?

　　When I wake up in my dream, it is you. You are my ubiquitous god.

　　Acacia has penetrated into the heart and lungs, strong, excited, excited, trembling, such as the stormy shore, can not be stopped, the heart dream is full of acacia.

　　I haven't received your reply yet. The time for letters to and from is too slow. The waiting time is long and people. I am tired of reading. When I look up, your gaze is in the green leaves of Phalaenopsis. Sprinkle water to green leaves, read the green branches in your house, two of a kind, that's all.

Wen Tianyu the music of our love. The music of harmony is sung by nightingales. Angel flutters on wings and flies under the moon. Silver glows down the ground. down the lily of the mountain that sank into dreamland. the moon dyed the mountain more secluded. Everything is immersed in the silence of satisfaction. I think your temporary silence is for the sake of your savings in the future, and everything will be released, lovers who fall in love!

We are about to set sail. There are beautiful clouds floating in the sky. The sea and sky are for us to soar. We are like an arrow from the string, shooting hope into the distance. Happiness is like splashing pearls and jade, like erupting fireworks in the night sky.

Let us persist, the way of life is inevitable, joys and sorrows, and tests, but if we love each other, we can overcome hardship. Let us be proud of each other, also a disaster and depression. Let your tenderness brush away my, also let my concern, ignore your sadness, let us tired, also tightly embrace together. Let us hold each other tightly and live together. Let you be my good wife, the loving mother of my children, and the good companion of our common friends.

I write to you from my wicker chair with a deep, sweet love for you.

Tonight, the moon is like practice, and we are in the same year, bathing in the ocean of love.

This is the late autumn when the leaves fall, the fallen leaves dance out the story of our love, and dance out the mature season of our two.

Imagine you reading my letters under the lamp, reading the poems we both loved together, or writing to me in the middle of the night when no one was whispering, and you felt incomparable happiness in your heart.

I would like to use my life's love, to hurt you, to you, let you free and comfortable, grow into the unrestrained growth of the mountain lily.

If there is a mountain full of flowers, I laugh in the bush.

Let me hold you in my arms tenderly and pityingly...

your crane,
Jianlong
November 14, 1989

剑龙：

本以为今生无缘再聚首，本以为缘来缘去，已在寂静之中幻灭了踪影，本以为彼此之间的恩怨已经了结，九年的相识相知，片刻的聚首相悦已经成为过去，两个多月前的结局是苍天的旨意，不曾怨天尤人。

谁知上苍怜我孤独，你又怜我寂寞，在我内外交困，心力交瘁的时候，你由珠海打来电话，那好像是遥远的天籁之音，似幻似真，我百感交集，不知是今生还是来世——这由天而降的幸福！

竹子何幸？幻海情缘，枯木又逢春。

上周六接你第一封信，信是莲姨托人亲自送来，找不到我，又打电话给兰姐，说是一封很重要的信，那时我正坐在兰姐对面，听到电话泪涌上我的眼眶——为了这位阿姨的善良与关爱。

这熟悉的字迹，这熟悉的名字和气息，我情不自禁地把它揸在胸前，好一会，才找一个无人的地方，把信读了一遍又一遍。

两日时间里，我读了又读，希望把你读得真切，希望读进你的深心。

星期日，我买了半斤毛线，用四支细细的针棒，开始织我的心丝，针针线线，织入我的惊喜，织入我的忧虑，织入我的思念。

今天又收到你接连的二封信，那倾注了火般热情，如潮汹涌，如岩溶喷发的言语，使我无法再保持沉默——喜极而泣，乐极生悲，若有一天再相失，一个人的日子将怎样面对？

因此我迟疑又迟疑，热情平静后，有无数的现实问题横亘在我俩面前：选择我，不知彼此要承受多久一样相思，两地情仇的生活？选择我，你将永远失去追逐其他青春美艳女子的机会；选择我，我只有我沉静，朴素的外表和一颗不服输的心；选择我，我怕太重感情而日后不能忍受爱人给我的委屈。或许我可以坦然面对世人对我的不公，却无法忍受最亲爱的人的责难，我愿给你时间，我愿你细细长长地考虑清楚，对于我，作为一个女子，能够轰轰烈烈地去爱，今天又蒙你如此厚待，已经无憾于青春，无憾于人生，若能让彼此再深深地相爱，我会无限感激而加倍地珍惜。

浮生若梦，富贵如云，我不会刻意去求，我只愿不生活得太贫困，生活得自自由由，漫漫人生，有一位相互信任、理解和扶持，相濡以沫的伴侣同行，一起欣赏春花夏艳，一起承受秋瑟冬寒，我已满足。

男女之间，获得爱易，若得敬难，我爱你，不为任何理由；我敬你，为了你的文才，你的大度，你的温柔，你对父母的孝顺，对世人的爱心。

目睹许多不幸的婚姻，对未来的婚姻心存畏惧，我是一位专心专意,死心塌地的女子,同时又是一位个性极强极烈的女子,我可以承受许多磨折,坦然面对困境,却没有能力去忍受亲人的伤害。

我很惶然,我怕再次失去

记得吗?这浅蓝色的情韵,这浅蓝色的海,这浅蓝色的爱的小舟——从今以后,百世共舟,让我握紧你的手!

好想共你开一支香槟,来贺你的文章获奖的喜悦。

你的竹子
1989年11月14日,故乡

Jianlong:

I thought that I would not be able to get together again in this life. I thought that the fate had come and gone, and I had been disillusioned in the silence. I thought that the feud between each other had ended. After nine years of acquaintance, the moment of gathering Prime Minister Yue had become a thing of the past. The ending more than two months ago was the will of heaven, and I never blamed God.

But God pity I am lonely, and you pity I am lonely. When I am in internal and external difficulties and exhausted, you call from Zhuhai, my, it seems to be a distant sound of nature, unreal or real. I have mixed feelings. I don't know whether it is in this life or in the afterlife –this happiness from nature!

How can bamboo be? Fantasy sea love, dead wood and spring.

I received your first letter last Saturday. The letter was sent by Aunt Lian's client in person. I couldn't find me, so I called Sister Lan and said it was a very important letter, I was sitting. Opposite to Sister, I heard the phone and tears welled up in my eyes–for the aunt's kindness and love.

This familiar handwriting, this familiar name and breath, I couldn't help covering it on my chest. After a while, I found a place where there was no one and read the letter 1 times and 1 times.

In the past two days, I have read and read, hoping to read you truly and read into your deep heart.

On Sunday, I bought half a kilo of wool and it with 4 thin needles rods. I began to weave my heart silk, needles and threads. weave my surprise, weave my worries and weave my thoughts.

Today, I received your 2 letter in succession, the words that poured fire-like enthusiasm, surging tide, and like karst eruption, so that I can no longer keep silent-tears of joy, joy begets sorrow, if one day lose, how will one face his life?

Therefore, I hesitated and hesitated. After the enthusiasm was calm, countless practical problems stood in front of us: choose me, I don't know how long we will have to bear the same love and hatred between the two places? Choose me, and you will never lose the chance to chase other young and beautiful women. Choose me, I only have my calm, simple appearance and a heart that does not admit defeat. Choose me, I am afraid I am too emotional and can't stand the injustice my lover will give me in the future. Perhaps I can calmly face the injustice of the world to me, but I can't bear the blame of my dearest. I would like to give you time. I would like you to think carefully and for a long time. For me, as a woman, I can love vigorously. Today, I have no regrets in youth and life. If I can make each other and deeply love each other again, I will be infinitely grateful and doubly cherish.

Floating life is like a dream, wealth is like a cloud, I will not

热爱生命
Love of Life

deliberately seek, I only wish not to live too poor, life is free, long life, there is a mutual trust, understanding and support, each other to a partner walk together, enjoy the spring flowers summer Yan, together to bear the autumn, winter cold, I have been satisfied.

Between men and women, it is easy to get love. If it is difficult to respect, I love you for no reason. I respect you for your literary talent, your tolerance, your gentleness, your filial piety to your parents and your love for the world.

Witnessing many unfortunate marriages, I am afraid of future marriages. I am the 1 dedicated and determined woman, and at the same time I am the 1 woman with a strong personality. I can bear many hardships and face difficulties calmly, but I have no ability to endure the harm of my relatives.

I'm scared, I'm afraid to lose again

Remember? the charm of this light blue, the sea of light blue, the boat of love that light blue-from now on, hundreds of generations of will together, let me hold your hand!

Good would like to open a champagne in your to congratulate you on the joy of winning your article.

Your bamboo
November 14, 1989, hometown

竹子：

　　这是11月6日开始每日一封的第十封信，我不竭的文思为你而牵。

　　张晓风写过：

　　"我们乃拥抱爱河的两岸，春天的时候，杨柳将两岸绿遍，河中有萍，河中有藻，河中有云影天光，而我，由此岸一经向你泅去，我正遇见你，自彼岸向我泅来，我们以同样柔和的倒映在青波里的柳条，在河心，千丝万缕的神秘地牵起手来，从此，在温柔得令人心痛的波心，我们相缠，握成永恒。

"我们已长成，因为有了相互的深爱，方知道明天风雨不太重要，因我们执手处张发可成风帆，高歌时，何妨倾山雨入盏，风雨因而不太重要，重要的是我们找到了一方可以共同承担风雨泥泞的肩……"

幸福是心灵的默契，是无私的奉献，是永远的忠诚。

伟大的心灵都必须经历过种种的磨难曲折，要经得起孤独寂寞，经得起困境和沉思苦索。幸福是要心地宽广，是永远不停地进取和适度的舒松，幸福就是简单的生活。

罗素的文字平实深远，尼采的哲学催人奋进，叔本华的悲观，而我喜欢的是乐观向上，潇洒轻盈。

人生往往是小人与英雄同台，良莠交织一起，不要太过偏执呵，何妨洒脱做人。

要学的很多，知识的海洋很深，但书读多时，与真正的智者圣贤对语，心中有无限的喜悦，书到用时总是恨少。

我愿不断追求，保有谦逊的态度，既享受人生，又将一颗心贴向自然，将灵魂化入自然的怀抱。

容我俩心连心。

凝望你，以深情万千
你的剑龙
1989年11月15日

Bamboo:

This is the tenth letter to be sent daily from November 6. My endless thoughts are for you.

Zhang Xiaofeng wrote:

热爱生命
Love of Life

"We are embracing both sides of the love river. In spring, willows will green both sides. There are in the river, algae in the river, and clouds and sky light in the river. As soon as I swim to you the bank, I am meeting you. swim to me from the other side of the. We reflect wicker in the green waves with the same softness, in the middle of the river, mysteriously hand in hand, from then on, in the tender heart-wrenching wave heart, we entangled, hold into eternity.

"We have grown up, because of our deep love for each other, we know that tomorrow's wind and rain are not very important, because we hold hands at Zhang Fa can the wind sail, singing, why not pour mountain rain into the, wind and rain is not very important, the important thing is that we have found a party can share the wind and rain muddy shoulder..."

Happiness is the tacit understanding of the soul, is selfless dedication, is always loyal.

The great mind must have gone through all kinds of hardships and twists and turns, to withstand loneliness and loneliness, to withstand difficulties and contemplation and bitter. Happiness is to be broad-minded, is always enterprising and moderate Shu Song, happiness is a simple life.

Russell's writing is plain and profound, Nietzsche's philosophy is inspiring, Schopenhauer's pessimism, and what I like is optimistic and light.

Life is often a small person and hero on the same stage, good and bad intertwined, don't be too paranoid, why not be free and easy.

There is a lot to learn and the ocean of knowledge is very deep, but when the book is read for long, it is to the language with the real wise sages, and there is infinite joy in my heart. When the book is used, I always hate less.

I am willing to continue to pursue, maintain a humble attitude, not only enjoy life, but also stick a heart to nature, and turn soul into the embrace of nature.

Let us both heart to heart.

Gazing at you with deep affection
Your Jianlong
November 15, 1989

剑龙：

我的爱人！

上星期六到今天，接连收到你的四封信，字里行间，满是切切情，绵绵意，如啼鹃的凄迷，每一封信我都反反复复地，不知读了多少次！直读到夜深，读到泪流，读入朦胧的境至。一张张素笺，如一瓣瓣情英，散落到我的枕畔鬓边，化作了缕缕情涟，化作片片云裳——我搂着这蓝莹莹的梦，搂着我的安详，搂着我一生的寄托。

这沉默后突然而来的情爱，如潮涌，如岩浆，冲破了我紧筑的心堤，溶化了厚厚的霜雪，竹子何幸？竟可以拥有一个男子汉全心全意的爱恋。

这深深的爱恋，这声声的呼唤，即使是铁石心肠的人，也会为之动容，我只不过是一个纤纤的女子，恐怕无福消受得了。在情爱面前，我不知说些什么，言语太苍白了，我唯有亮起双眸，凝视着你，遐想着期待着你的仙临。关山万里，我的爱人，何日是归程？

手中的毛线，一团团，一圈圈，针针线线，分分秒秒，全是我无言的思念，无声的渴求，君心妾意，岂敢负相思

Love of Life

意！我不知如何述说，我无法井然安排，我思绪万千却又空蒙无依，佛说：修百世方能同舟，修千世方可同眠，你我可是千百世的缘分？

金钱何价？富贵何价？我为着一个情字，痴痴迷迷了二十几年，唯恐世俗的尘埃污染了它的圣洁，二十几年的寻寻觅觅，只有你知道我坚强的外表下，包着一颗何等脆弱的心。这是一颗需要呵护，需要理解的心呵！这颗心柔情万顷，风情万种，这颗心执着、痴绝，这颗心从今以后，只属于你！

拿去吧，我的爱人，从此，有一副柔弱的肩膀会同你共担风雨，共跋泥泞，愿我俩之间凡事相信，凡事忍耐，凡事包容，凡事希望，不要再一个人苦苦支撑了。

不要给我太多的宠爱，不要对我期望过高，如果有一天你不再爱我，我会悄然离去，你永远是我潇洒的爱人，我不会用家庭，道德的绳索将你缚住。我只怕这几年，无法像常人一样，侍奉在你跟前，我只怕你过分的凄清，冷落，只怕关山万里，阻了归程，原谅我呵，我不得不离开这片土地，暂时离开你，令你长久地思念，长久地将我等待。

前路是一片泥泞，选择我，可苦了你！

你的竹子

1989年11月15日

Jianlong:

My love!

From last Saturday to today, I have received 4 letters from you one after another. Between the lines, they are full of earnest feelings and continuous meanings, like the sadness of crowing cuckoo. I have read each letter over and over again, and I do not know how many times I have read it! Read straight into the night, read the tears, read into the hazy to the. Zhang Su's notes, like petals of love English, scattered on my pillow sideburns, turned into wisps of love, turned into pieces of clouds-I hug this blue dream, hug my peace, hug my life's sustenance.

This silence after the sudden love, such as the tide, such as magma, broke through my tightly built heart the embankment, melting the thick frost and snow, bamboo lucky? It is possible to have a man's whole-hearted love.

This deep love, this call, even a stone-hearted person, will be moved by it, I am just a slender woman, I am afraid there is no blessing to be able to stand it. In front of love, I don't know what to say. My words are too pale. I can only light up my eyes and stare at you, daydreaming about the of your fairy. Guanshan Wanli, my love, when is the return journey?

The wool in my hand, a ball, a circle, a needle thread, every minute, is all my silent thoughts, silent desire, your heart concubine meaning, how dare you negative acacia meaning! I don't know how to say it. I can't arrange it properly. I have a lot of thoughts but I have no way to. Buddha said: only when you cultivate a hundred generations can you be in the same boat, when you cultivate a thousand can you sleep together. you and I are the fate a thousand generations?

What is the price of money? What is the price of wealth? I have been obsessed with a word of love for more than 20 years, lest the worldly dust pollute its holiness. After more than 20 years of searching, only you know how fragile my heart 1 under my strong appearance. This is the 1 heart that needs care and understanding! This heart is tender and sentimental. This heart is persistent and infatuated.

热爱生命
Love of Life

From now on, this heart belongs only to you!

Take it, my love. From now on, there is a pair of weak shoulders that will share the wind and rain you, and the and postscript are muddy. wish to us believe in everything, endure everything, tolerate everything, hope everything, and stop supporting alone.

Don't give me too much love, don't expect too much of me, if one day you no longer love me, I will quietly leave, you will always be my natural and unrestrained lover, I will not use the family, moral rope will you bound. I am afraid that over the past few years, I cannot serve you like ordinary people. I am afraid that your is too and desolate. I am afraid that Guan Shan Wanli has blocked return. Forgive me. I have to leave this land and leave you temporarily, which makes you miss me for a long time and wait for me for a long time.

The road ahead is muddy, choose me, but bitter you!

Your bamboo
November 15, 1989

剑龙：

一日一封信，你会把我宠坏的，在分离的日子里，你的信将会长伴我身旁，信，给我几许甜蜜，几许辛酸？有情的是你，无情的也是你，即使你拒绝了我的日子，我还是翘首以待，待那悄然而至的话语，我，一位从感情的低谷走了出来的女子，双眸又再溢满秋波，脸颊又再焕发光彩，心里柔情万顷，我的冤家，我命中注定的原来是你！

我逃不脱呵，逃不脱你汹涌的情潮。我想你念你醒时梦中都是你，我不再矜持，不再骄傲，不再孤独苦撑，不再要华衣锦食金屋虚荣，也不要世人的认可！我只要你的温厚笑容，你善良的心地，你的智慧，你的进取，你的从容自适，你的隐世情怀。你积极的处世，是我舍不去的终身追寻，这追寻，尽管几经挫折，遍染尘埃，尽管得失几度，踌躇几番，可命中注定，你是我终生的爱人，如寒梅之傲霜，历久弥坚，如滴水之穿石，历久弥深。

未来，有一方空白天地由我俩去创拓，我俩年轻，我俩勤奋，我俩聪明，有爱的力量，我俩完全有能力经得起贫寒，耐得起富贵，我俩既有创造阳春白雪的境界，又有承受咸鱼白菜的勇气，我俩既超脱又现实，既积极又随遇而安，我俩的心灵有一方留白的天地，那里永远有春花鸟语，温情脉脉，有世间万种风情。

问世间情是何物，直教生死相许？

我的一生，因为有了你的真诚深爱而无悔无憾！

我身边都是些至情至性的朋友，兰姐虽饱受人生困苦和不幸婚姻的折磨，仍是鼓励我追求真爱；阿吟舍去多次出国嫁富翁的机会，而与一位重情义的男子结为终身伴侣，她安详的笑容里，有着一份圣母般的灵光；阿娟虽认识了一位比较富有的男子，在江门为好买了房子，但她幸运出国求学的机会，却在激烈地动摇他俩的关系，她仍然是心未所属，怕委屈了自己的一生。

爱是生命里永恒的主题，我俩得到的岂止是结果？我俩将努力保持自己的清新，自己的本性，改正自己顽劣的脾性，我希望自己永远通情达理，永远是贤妻，永远和着你进取的脚步，永远处于追求之中，你是我永远追求的爱人。

人生不如意事十常八九，家事已经渐渐解决。表姐会于十月上旬赴港定居，将定居指标先让给她，为他人做嫁衣裳。身边的好友一个又一个地走了，娟去了加拿大，吟去了挪威，她们就这样悄悄地走，只有我一个消消停停，行期在不定

热爱生命
Love of Life

之中，要你长久地将我等待，真不知有多少不忍、无奈，多少泪！

这世间，唯有你肯长久地将我等待，我怕这一生欠你太多，我不知如何的回报。

君心妾意，曾经沧海难为水，除却巫山不是云，不要思念我太苦，该跳舞时还是去跳舞，该散步时去散步，该呼朋唤友时，还是去投入朋友之欢笑之中。

初冬乍寒，冷暖自重！

念你的竹子
1989 年 11 月 16 日

Jianlong:

A letter a day, you will spoil me. In the days of separation, your letter will accompany me. How sweet and bitter will you give me? It is you who are sentient, and it is you who are heartless. Even if you refuse my day, I am still waiting for the words that come quietly. I, 1 a woman who came out from the trough of feelings, my eyes are full of autumn waves again, my cheeks are radiant again, and my heart is tender. My enemy, I was destined to be you!

I can't escape, I can't escape the surging tide you. I think you think that when you wake up, you are all in your dreams. I am no longer reserved, no longer proud, no longer lonely and bitter, no longer want to the vanity of the golden house in the of China,, food,, and no recognition from the world! I only want your gentle smile, your kind heart, your wisdom, your enterprising, your calm and self-adaptation, your hidden feelings. Your active life in the world is a lifelong pursuit that I cannot give up. this pursuit, despite several setbacks, times stained with dust, despite several gains and losses, and several hesitations, can fate. You are my lifelong lover, such as the proud frost of the cold plum, which will last longer and longer, and the will last longer and longer, such as the stone of dripping water.

In the future, there will be a blank world where I to Chuangtuo. We are young, we are diligent, we are smart and have the power of love. We are fully capable of withstanding poverty, of withstanding and honor. We have both the to create a state of sunshine and snow, and the courage to bear salted fish and cabbage. We are both detached and realistic, both active and comfortable with the situation. Our hearts have a world left blank, there will always be spring flowers and birds, tender feelings, there are ten thousand kinds of customs in the world.

Ask what love is in the world and teach life and death to live and die together?

My whole life, because of your sincere love and no regrets!

I am surrounded by friends who are most affectionate and sexual. Although Lanjie suffers from hardships in life and unfortunate marriage, she still encourages me to pursue true love. A Yin gave up many opportunities to go abroad to marry a rich man and became a lifelong partner with 1 a man who attached great importance to friendship. her and serene smile, she 1 a virgin–like aura. Although Ajuan met 1 richer men, she bought a house for the good in Jiangmen, but her lucky opportunity to study abroad was shaking their relationship fiercely. She still did not belong her heart and was afraid of wronging her whole life.

Love is the eternal theme of life. is the we get? We will try our best to keep our freshness, our nature and correct our stubborn temperament. I hope I will always be reasonable, a good wife, always

热爱生命
Love of Life

follow your enterprising steps, and always be in pursuit. You are the lover I will always pursue.

Nine times out of ten things in life, family affairs have been gradually solved. My cousin will settle in Hong Kong in early October, and will give her the settlement index first to make wedding clothes for others. The good friends around me left one after another. went to Canada and Yin went to Norway. They just walked quietly. I was the only one who stopped and stopped. The travel period was uncertain. I really don't know how many tears you can't bear to wait for me for a long time!

In this world, only you are willing to wait for me for a long time. I am afraid I owe you too much in my life. I do not know how to repay.

Jun Xin concubine meaning, once the sea was difficult for water, except Wushan is not a cloud, don't miss me too hard, to dance or go to dance, to go for a walk when, to to call friends, or to put into the laughter of friends.

Early winter cold at first, cold and warm self-weight!

Miss your bamboo
November 16, 1989

剑龙：

你的竹子又禁不住回复从前一样的等待，今日收到你的第六封信，你周日写的。

每次收信是读了又读，中午由于读信而不肯睡觉，初读时，心跳脸红，那感觉好像第一次把手交给你相拥跳舞时，刻骨铭心，不知道何来十八岁女子怀春的情怀，再读三读时，幸福的感觉之中夹着轻愁，这轻愁日浓，你这样爱我，累吗？会不会感到美中不足？请你细审你的追求，我是一位优缺点都很明显的女子，只是比同龄人多了点经历，少年时多一些磨折，不值得你如此深爱的呵！

本已收拾心情不再恋爱，将来顺其自然去完成人生的必经，可是在我尘缘未绝的时候，你深爱的情潮汹涌而至，我游不出你这深深的海洋。

我知道，这一生若没有你的爱，生命的田原会很荒芜，但大地无垠，有沃土就必然有荒原，无论这块土地如何荒芜，我都会辛勤地耕耘，把一切的遭遇都视作必然，怎样的过程都会努力去面对。如今这片土地，因你的爱的甘露，阳光，辛劳，爱与希望的种子又在萌芽，那一片嫩绿，显出了怵然的生机。

原谅我的忧愁，或许，幸福之中总是夹着轻愁。从接你的电话那天起，就暗暗数着你的归期，见不着你，那幸福之感总觉得飘然。

你来还是我去，相见时难别亦难，东风无力百花残，昨夜西风凋碧树，独上高楼，望尽天涯路，明月关山阻隔，断肠人在天涯！

与你共舞后，在故乡再也提不起热情应酬舞约，忆我俩舞时的辉煌，世上舞者，能达我俩如痴如醉的境界的，能有几个？

春花夏日秋月冬雪，本是恒定的轮回，而我俩的感情历练，经过了秋瑟冬寒，该是春暖花开时节。不知爱你，何日是尽头？

你因何如此信任我？你凭什么如此长久地，将我来等待？好想你呵，却见不着。

毛衣织了近一周，手工不敢夸，花式花样是一学就会，好希望自己是个心灵手巧的女子,但我不是,感激你的包容——我的全部。

夜深了,只我案前一盏灯亮着,又回复了往日灯下娓娓地向你倾诉。如此良夜,世上有多少女子,在笺上向心上人诉说心怀呢?

驿寄梅花,鱼传尺素,砌成此情无重数。

好想你呵!

你的竹子
1989 年 11 月 17 日

Jianlong:

Your bamboo can't help but reply to the same wait as before. I received your sixth letter today, you wrote Sunday.

Every time I received the letter, I read it again and again. I refused to sleep at noon because of reading the letter. When I first read it, my heart blushed. that felt as if I the first time I gave you my hand to hug and dance. I don't know how the 18-year-old woman's feelings of huaichun came from. When I read 3 again, the feeling of happiness was filled with light sorrow and. this light sorrow strong, tired? Will not feel the United States? Please carefully examine your pursuit. I am the 1 woman with obvious advantages and disadvantages. I just have a little more experience than my peers and have more twists and turns when I was a teenager. I am not worthy of your deep love!

I have already cleaned up my mood and stopped falling in love. I will let nature take its course to complete the necessary course of life in the future. However, when my fate is not over, the tide of your deep love is surging, I can swim out of your deep ocean.

I know that without your love in this life, the fields of life will be very barren, but the land is boundless, there will be wasteland if there is fertile soil. No matter how barren this land is, I will work hard and regard all the encounters as inevitable. I will try my best to face the process. Now this land, because of the nectar of your love, sunshine, toil, the seeds of love and hope are budding again, and that green, showing the vitality of timid.

Forgive my sorrow, perhaps, happiness is always sandwiched with light sorrow. From the day I answered your phone, I secretly counted your return date. Without seeing you, I always felt happy.

You come or I go, it is difficult to see each other when we meet, the east wind is weak and the flowers are all over the place, last night the west wind withered the green trees, alone on the tall buildings, looking at the end of the world, the bright moon is blocked by the mountains, and the heartbroken people are at the end of the world!

After dancing with you, I can no longer afford to have a warm social party in my hometown. I remember the glory of our dance. How many dancers in the world can be intoxicated with us?

Spring flowers, summer, autumn moon, winter snow, this is a constant cycle, and our emotional experience, after autumn, winter and cold, it should be the spring season. I do not know love you, when is the end?

Why do you trust me so much? Why did you wait so long for me? I miss you so much, but I can't see you.

Sweaters have been knitted and for nearly a week. I dare not boast about the craftsmanship. I can learn fancy patterns as soon as I learn them. I wish I were a clever woman, but I am not. I am grateful for your tolerance–all of me.

热爱生命
Love of Life

Late at night, only I a light on in front of the case, and then replied to the old days and confided to you under the light. On such a good night, how many women in the world tell their hearts to their hearts on their notes?

Post send plum blossom, fish pass ruler element, build this feeling without weight.

I miss you so much!

Your bamboo
17 November 1989

剑龙：

相思本是无凭语，还向花笺费泪行。

昨日止，已收到你每日一封沉甸甸的信，想到你孤灯之下疾书的情景，血似的浓情，化作声声呼唤，那份幸福，渗着痛楚，渗着朝思暮想，渗着柔情，深深地萦绕着我，一切的委屈，酸楚，怨悔都融化于这无边的真爱之中。

我是怀着怎样的柔情将你思念？情到深处人孤独，相思之苦，明月清风代做证。一样花开为底迟？我心中的那丛秋菊，终于为你怒放！

谢你的相知，谢你的信任，谢你男子汉的自信，谢你的深爱，谢你甘霖雨露的滋润！你已是我心灵的唯一领主，在经过风刀霜剑严相迫之后，她已完全为你开放。有缘的终将成为终身相许的伴侣！

我俩的交往，都已活在记忆，好像没有开始，也没有结束，一切源于盘古初开，绵于地老天荒，过往的曲折，未来的考验，都有一股神力将我俩牵引，冥冥之中，都有一颗同样的心为彼此跳动。

我极之珍惜这份情，唯恐世俗的尘埃将它污染，你是我幽谷之中的那株蓝草,那样晶莹,素洁,那样倔强,坚烈,我的圣主呵,原来你就是我的梦幻,我的现实,我的红尘及我的空灵!

沉寂多年,都只是为了今天生命之中灵与肉的结合。

恨不能乘风而去,恨不能月夜伴君夜读,恨这山太高,水太长,恨白云悠悠,恨过尽千帆皆不是。

十一月将尽,琐事缠身,希望能尽快抽身到珠海,过几日属于我俩的日子。

爱你的,

竹子

1989年11月19日

Jianlong:

Acacia is without words, but also to spend tears line.

the end of yesterday's, I have received a heavy letter from you every day. When I think of the scene of your writing under the lonely lamp, the blood-like feeling turns into a voice calling. The happiness is with pain, with thoughts, with tenderness, deeply haunting me. All grievances, soreness, regrets melt into this boundless true love.

With what tenderness do I miss you? Deep down, people are lonely and suffer from lovesickness. The bright moon and cool breeze prove on behalf of. Is the same flower blooming late? The autumn chrysanthemum in my heart is finally in full bloom for you!

Thank you for knowing each other, thank you for your trust, thank you for your man's confidence, thank you for your deep love, thank you for the rain and dew! You are the only lord of my heart, and after being by the wind and the sword, she is fully open to you. The one who is predestined friends will eventually become a lifelong companion!

Our relationship has already lived in memory, it seems that

热爱生命
Love of Life

there is no beginning or end. Everything comes from the beginning of Pangu, from the end of the world. The twists and turns of the past and the tests of the future all have a divine force pulling us. In the dark, both have the same heart beating for each other.

I cherish this feeling very much, lest secular dust pollute it. You are the bluegrass in my valley, so crystal clear, simple, stubborn, strong and, my holy Lord, so you are my dream, my reality, my world of mortals and my ethereal!

Silence for many years, all just for the combination of spirit and flesh in today's life.

I wish I couldn't ride the wind, I wish I couldn't accompany you on the moonlit night to read night, hate mountain is too high, water is too long, hate white clouds leisurely, hate over all thousands of sails.

November is coming to an end and I am busy with trivial matters. I hope I can get out of Zhuhai as soon as possible and live a few days that belong to us.

Love you,

Bamboo

November 19, 1989

竹子：

　　我的爱人。

　　让你久等了。

　　连接收你三封回信，喜不自禁，你热烈真挚的回应，宛如交响乐之中的和音，震撼了我的灵魂！

　　收你第一封信时，我脸如火烧，一种从未有过的妙感由心间升起，心跳得很响很快。

　　自以为冷静，竟是如此的狂乱，爱的魔力不可抵挡，握着你的信，舍不得拆开，冲上宿舍，小心翼翼挑开信封，读到了你的柔情万缕。我还没细看你的情潮，已是热泪盈眶，这颗未曾完全交出过的情心，仍是洁如夏荷，挺如劲松，我二十多岁的生命，小心地培植这株爱苗，紧拥着它，就是为了此刻，在这样一个俊美的年华，将它毫无保留地交给你，从此我俩相属，我俩携手风雨同路，心心相印，让爱情卧成一脉青山，长绿在自然的怀抱。

喜悦之情在我心间，爱情可入诗入酒入梦，又一次印证了，我的身心散发着的宁恬幸福的馨香。

碧云天，故乡情，今宵月色应如水，我眺望远方，沐浴在爱的柔情蜜意之中，幸运之神抚我脸颊，引出不绝如缕的情思，即使此刻，我仍是止不住满心的喜悦，任心狂跳，任泪横飞，任血沸腾，任思绪如脱缰的野马，奔驰原野，追逐蓝空……

我如何表达我心声于万一？我以温柔的手指，弹拨爱情的清音，让缠绵、激越、傲昂、低回的旋律交相鸣奏，缤纷的音符，疾缓的节拍，流泻出烂漫的乐章！任我俩智慧的笔，画出我俩最新最美的图画，笔端勾勒出异彩，蕴含诗意，勾出现实，勾出梦幻，要比琼瑶笔下的爱情更加现实，要用这一生，来书写我俩的挚爱。

本要给你电话，谁知你先我而打，你总是那个敢作敢为，富于行动的女子。知道你即将来珠海续缘，心中十分激动欢喜。这一次将会是一次全新的体验。

我相信，我俩的合力一定可以战胜人生的苦难。

当泪落尽了，我俩的爱，又升起了希望的艳阳！

将你紧紧拥抱……

剑龙
1989 年 11 月 21 日

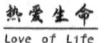
Love of Life

Bamboo:

    My lover.

    Thank you for waiting.

    Even receiving the 3 reply from your, I couldn't help but you a warm and sincere response, just like the harmony in a symphony, which shocked my soul!

    When I received your first letter, my face was burning. 1 was a wonderful feeling that I had never felt before. rose from heart, and my heart beat very loudly and quickly.

    I think I am calm, but I am so crazy. The magic of love is irresistible. Holding your letter, I am reluctant to open the and rush to the dormitory. I carefully open the envelope and read your tender feelings. I haven't looked closely at your love tide, tears are already in my eyes. This love, which has not been fully handed over, is still and, such as Xia He, and is quite like Jin Song. In my twenties, I carefully cultivated this love seedling and held it tightly, just to give it to you unreservedly at this moment, in such a beautiful time. From then on, we belong to each other, we hand in hand wind and rain on the same road, heart to heart, let love lie into a pulse of green hills, long green in the embrace of nature.

    Joy is in my heart, love can be into the poem into the wine into the dream, once again confirmed, my body and mind exudes the fragrance of happiness.

    Blue sky, hometown feeling, this night moon color should be like water, I look into the distance, bathed in the tender feelings of love, lucky god caressed my cheek, lead to endless thoughts, even at this moment, I still can't help but full of joy, let the heart jump, let tears fly, let blood boil, let thoughts like runaway wild horses, galloping wilderness, chasing the blue sky...

How do I express my heart in case? With my gentle fingers, I plucked the unvoiced sound of love, and let lingering, agitated, proud, low back melody sing, colorful notes, slow beat, flow out the brilliant movement! Let us draw our latest and most beautiful pictures with our wise pen. The pen outlines the splendor, contains poetry, outlines the reality and outlines the dream. It is more realistic than Qiong Yao's love. It is necessary to use this life to write our love.

I was going to call you, but you called me first and. You are always the woman who is bold and full of action. I am very excited and happy to know that you are coming to Zhuhai to continue your. This time will be a new experience.

I believe that we can overcome the sufferings of life together.

When tears fell, our love, and the sun of hope rose!

Hold you tight...

Jianlong
21 November 1989

剑龙：

晨起，一阵清新的气息涌入心中，原来所有的昨日，都是为了今天的回报。

爱一个人，是不需要理由，爱你，是风霜赐予的成熟，我宁馨的心瓣为你展开。

我相信，只要你肯去做，一定会有能力做好，我的关注，是你挫折之时的信心，倦时的歌音及胜时的掌声，无论是怎样的相守或分离，一生一世都跟定了你，死心塌地。想不到，在叶终于落尽的深秋，生命赋予我俩全新的意义。

案前的绿叶记载着我俩的悲喜，一切景语皆情语，人间因有

热爱生命
Love of Life

爱，我因遇着你，日子便显得安然而有趣意，今日的天籁是分外的悦耳动听，我的烦恼，焦躁不安，因为有你的气定神闲而宁静。

琐事虽多，也阻不了我渴见你的行动，希望可以尽快见面。

想念你！

竹子

1989年11月22日

Jianlong:

In the morning, a fresh breath poured into my heart. It turned out that all yesterday was for today's return.

Love a person, is do not need reason, love you, is the wind and frost bestowed maturity, my heart is open for you.

I believe that as long as you are willing to do it, you will have the ability to do it well. My concern is your confidence when you are frustrated, the of songs when you are tired and, and the applause when you are and. No matter how you stay or separate, you will follow you 1 your whole life. Unexpectedly, in the late autumn when the leaves finally fell, life gave us a new meaning.

The green leaves in front of the case record our joys and sorrows. All scenery words are love words. The world is because of love. When I meet you, the days look safe and interesting. Today's sounds of nature are extra and pleasant to the ear. My worries and restlessness are because of your calm and tranquility.

Although there are many trivial things, I can't stop my thirst to see your actions. I hope to meet you as soon as possible.

Miss you!

Bamboo

22 November 1989

竹子：

可好？

毛衣织好了？你丝丝的情意，都在其中了。

今夜月圆人不圆，如此良夜，只想邀你共赏，一同醉倒！

夜来读书风满天，或是画眉深浅入时无？

我恋我俩的深挚，我恋我俩爱的清音，如今迈步从头越，从头越，江山如旧，残阳如血。文学的瑰丽和绮迷，令我痴痴地醉，只恨不成书痴。

等待你的翩临。

我俩必将长相牵……

剑龙
1989 年 11 月 23 日

Bamboo:

Okay?

Did you knit the sweater? Your affection is all in it.

Tonight the moon is full and the people are not round. On such a good night, I just want to invite you to enjoy it together and get drunk together!

Night reading wind all over the sky, or thrush depth into the time?

I in love with our deep feelings, and I in love with our unvoiced love. Now I am stepping from beginning to end, from beginning to end, the country is like the old, and the sun is like blood. The magnificence of literature and the of yee fans make me crazy drunk, only hate not books crazy.

Waiting for your Pian Pro.

We will both look ...

Jianlong
23 November 1989

竹子思念剑龙心切，告了一周的假期，于十一月二十七日来珠海会见爱郎。

那日清晨，剑龙早早起床到车站去接竹子。情人就要到了，剑龙心情激动，想象即将见面的情景，秋风吹过来，都化作了暖融融的春意。车子入站了，窗口挥着一只手——那正是剑龙要等的竹子！

竹子下了车，剑龙快步上前，也不怕难为情，俩人便在人群之中紧紧地拥抱在一起！今夕何夕，今夕何年，相爱的男女，曾经经历了多少艰辛曲折，才有此刻久别的重逢？刹那间，泪水从竹子眼中夺眶而出，剑龙也泪盈于睫，真是百感交集，一言难尽。

"总算把你盼来了，好高兴。"剑龙说。

"见不着你心里不踏实，拥抱着你感觉是如此不同！"竹子道。

"一夜旅途辛苦了吧？"剑龙怜惜地理理竹子的秀发。

"还好，只是因想念你整夜不眠！"

"回去先洗个热水澡，养养神，然后去饮茶，今天周末，阿刚一班朋友开茶位在等我们。"

剑龙将竹子带回宿舍。剑龙独自住在一个套间，床子不大，但能够有俩人独处的空间，竹子暗暗开心，心头的大石也放下了，因为之前一直担心这次在珠海时的住所，若同其他同事同处一室就会不方便。

洗过澡，换上宽宽的睡衣，室内播着邓丽君的歌，正轻轻唱着《甜蜜蜜》，剑龙在为花草修剪浇水，竹子望着他专注的神情，心里甜柔舒畅，守得云开见月明，应该就是这种心境吧？她轻轻地闭着倦眼。

竹子倦极而眠，直到阿刚来电话："剑龙，可接到竹子？大家都到齐了，就等你俩，莫非正在春宵一刻值千金？"

"你不要乱说！她到了，倦极而眠，你们先吃，我俩半小时左右就到。"

收了线，竹子不知何时已起床，洗过脸，抹上唇膏，颊上有着清新润泽的气息，令人眼前一亮——好一个如花的女子！

剑龙赞道："竹子你很漂亮，天生丽质。"

竹子笑了笑："睡了一阵，精神好了，要不怎敢见人？初次相见，要是来了个丑八怪，把朋友吓着，丢了你的脸就惨了。"

"那里的话，这么漂亮的女孩子，君子好逑，他们赞都来不及。"

"又口花花，快些去吧，不然你的兄弟们等急了。"

到银都酒店餐厅，已经是上午十一时，大家一见面，就赞开了。六尺多高，玉树临风的阿刚伸过手来同竹子相握："我是阿刚，欢迎你来珠海，剑龙真有福气，交了个文如其名的女子。竹子，正好是修长清雅的。"

"一头长长秀发柔情似水，潇洒！"阿强说，回望了一眼身边剪着齐耳短发的女友阿霞。阿霞笑道："他很少赞人，他要说美就真是美，我很喜欢竹子的粉红色长裙，正好托出上这娇柔的身姿。"

剑龙开心地笑着，竹子甜在心里，那身材胖胖的阿东不知从哪里现身，插了一句："我说竹子的气质最好，斯文大方，人见人爱！"

一听见他说"人见人爱"，大家都哗哗地哄笑起来，都说这肥仔色胆包天，见了靓女就情不自禁，连自己兄弟的女友也有非分之想，日后可别要发花痴了！"

阿东真是哭笑不得，竹子道："阿东也不过是赞我而已，养成好气质是很难的事，希望自己配得上大家的称赞，剑龙时常向我提起你们，今天见面我实在是十分高兴，请各位日后多关照。"

大家又喧嚷了一番，才开始饮茶。

竹子的应对大方得体，人又长得灵气端秀，看来朋友都很喜欢她加入圈子。

剑龙的兄弟都很正直真诚，物以类聚，人以群分，都是些值得相交的朋友。

不愧是同龄人，席间谈谈笑笑，时间飞一般过去，都吃饱喝足了，将近下午二时，阿刚结了账，提议去海滨公园，大家同意，一行人上了公共汽车。

珠海的马路真是宽阔，六辆车并着行驶也没有问题，一路上都是花草树木，是名副其实的花园城市，清新的空气吹进车里，竹子愉快地呼吸着。大家在谈笑，车子经过九洲大道、珠海宾馆、石景山，停在海滨公园门前。

海滨公园里有一片葱葱的树林，对面石景山上美石嶙峋，乳白色的别墅群点缀在树影之间，好像人间仙境，中午的一场骤雨将山显得更绿，雨后出岫的云是飘荡着的棉花，依依地绕着山峰飘游。

行入林中小径，高佬刚说："很久没来这里了，看这些树越长越高，越长越密，差点连路都找不到了。"

"吹牛，你那么多女朋友，整天在拍拖，怕是你对这里每一株草都了如指掌。"肥东笑他。

"我是粗人，哪里有那么浪漫？剑龙是机关里著名的才子，诗词歌赋，文采风流，才配在这些青山绿水里谈情说爱。

如今有了竹子，才子佳人，真是令人羡慕！"

大家笑了起来，阿霞道："正是，我就没有这个福气了，阿强从来没有带我来公园，不懂浪漫，唉。"

"也不是这么说，阿强的厨艺可是大家公认的，把阿霞养得珠圆玉润的，这么美丽，比逛公园强多了。"剑龙道。

阿强喜道："剑龙说得对，若不嫌弃，找个时间请你和竹子到舍下一聚，试试我的小菜，看我可不是凭空将美女追到手的。"

"咦，怎么不请我和阿刚？大细超，不行不行！"阿东嚷道。

"当然是大家都来，看看我俩如何双剑合璧！"阿霞在空中做了个舞剑的手势，大伙又是哄笑一通。

来到珠海渔女的塑像前，微笑着的渔女，站立在海中央，双掌托起一颗明珠，托起了珠海人民勤劳丰收的喜悦。

大伙散开活动，剑龙和竹子坐在一块有点潮湿的礁石上，浅黄色的海水一浪一浪地涌上来，拍击礁石，溅起串串水花，有些还打到俩人的身上，秋阳下，风又凉又暖地吹拂着脸颊，撩起竹子的秀发，几朵白云在天上舒卷，海里有人游泳，像鱼一般在水里浮动，岸上几个孩子在放风筝。

剑龙轻轻地拥着竹子，听着海潮的低吟浅唱，心情是难得的轻松舒畅，竹子说："你这班朋友真好，有情有义，风趣幽默，同他们一起真是好开心。"

"大家相交也快十年了，一起成长，彼此了解，感情确实深厚，日后要是离开他们，一定会依依不舍。"

"我明白，只是人生无不散的筵席，有些东西该放手时就要放手，有缘的总有一日再相聚。"

见剑龙有些伤感，竹子说："阿刚很欣赏你。人也很豪爽，你和他可谓诗心剑侠。"

"我和他感情最好,比兄弟还亲,别看他高大英挺,其实也有很细心的时候,所以他的女朋友像走马灯,数也数不完。不知哪一个才是真的。"剑龙道。

"阿东特别风趣幽默,他可拍拖了?"

"拍了几个都没成功,嫌他胖,不久就散了,其实他内心很纯良,相处了会知道他的可爱。"

"阿强同阿霞好合拍,好有夫妻相。"

"是,他们就快要结婚,阿强为人最诚挚踏实,交托给他的事情最有把握,是值得长久相交的朋友。至于阿霞,处事大方得体,风趣幽默,俩人实在好匹配。"

谈着谈着,不知不觉晚霞已在西天飘散,树叶颤动着,正在散走一天的热气,也是,作了一天大伞的荫凉,美化园林,凉爽了游人,也该舒展一下疲惫的筋骨了,一宿过后,又要重复同样的工作。点点归帆披着落霞回航……

"黄昏的景色真美呵!夕阳无限好。"竹子说。

"很快就到月上柳梢头,人约黄昏后了,"剑龙提议:"要不要去海边走走?"

"好!"

然后,竹子挽着剑龙的臂膀,沿着海岸,沐着海风漫行,晚风中,浪花拍岸的声音越见温柔,一群海鸥在岸上翻飞嬉戏,在俩人周围掠过,渐渐地,他俩融入了沙滩上霭霭的暮色之中。

朋友们见他俩兴致还浓,便先告辞回府,剑龙俩人在海滩上又留下了一行又一行的足迹,直走到天上亮起月儿,亮起满天星光,走到肚子饿了,才去海边侨苑酒店餐厅用晚饭。

这里的灵芝乳鸽最出名,鸽子先用灵芝调好的味料拌好,再红烧,味道都已渗入体肉里,用橘汁点,真是吃过回味无穷,又有药效,是秘制的招牌菜。除此,东江盐焗鸡和鲜鱼茜葱豆腐汤也很好,再要一碟蒜蓉白菜仔,一壶寿眉热茶,坐在临窗望海的餐桌上,也是一种享受。

俩人饿了,菜一端上来就开吃。

剑龙问:"菜的味道如何?"

"好好味,这灵芝鸽,让我齿颊留香,回味无穷。"

"所以我每次来都会叫这道菜,个个都赞好吃。"

"有没有外卖,我想带两只回去给兰姐试试。"

"一定会有,让我来安排。"

晚餐后,沿着长长的景山道漫行,已快十点的马路行人稀少,夜很静,秋空高爽,空气清新,令人呼吸特别畅快。夜风有点凉,竹子将身子靠近剑龙,眉宇间透出无限温柔,她说:"龙,我今天真是很开心很舒畅,谢谢你及你的朋友。"

"我也很久没试过这么开心了,你给我们带来欢乐。"

"情人、好友、妙景、美食,人生能这样度过,也是一种幸运。"

……

回到宿舍,洗过澡,已经是午夜时分,夜深了,人们大多都已经沉入了梦乡,夜凉如水,周遭显得好宁静好宁静。

剑龙放着恋人浪漫曲,《爱情故事》一曲在耳边轻轻响起,在心头萦回,竹子躺卧在床上,脸上泛着红晕,星目迷离,剑龙关了顶灯,拧亮台灯,调出柔和的光线,然后坐到床上,情深款款地望着竹子:"你洗完澡的样子,如清水出芙蓉,比梨花一枝春带雨的杨贵妃还美。"

一起沐浴后,回到床上,身心有说不出的畅快,浑身每一个细胞都在诉说着爱情。

竹子说:"真是太美妙了,那快感是如临仙境,收缩的一刹已成永恒!"

"原来这就是灵与肉结合的最高境界。"剑龙道。

"女人有这个宝贝,男人怎么抵挡?"

"所以才有窈窕淑女,君子好逑。"

"怪不得男人都这么好色。"

"想不到你这书生会这么强劲。"

竹子枕在剑龙的臂弯,谈着谈着就进入了梦乡,剑龙看着她蔷薇色的脸颊和满足的面容,嗅着她发端散着的淡淡幽香,也很快沉入了梦乡,夜温柔,月光照进窗户,静静洒在这一对爱人的身上,不由得发出了会心的微笑……

当东方破晓,竹子在剑龙的凝望的笑容中苏醒过来,一夜无梦的甜睡,令她越发显得娇艳,恋爱中的女人是最美丽的,此刻她深深感受到了,她深情望着剑龙,心里充满了幸福的感觉。

接下来六天的时间,已分不出晨昏日夜,他俩在情欲的波峰浪谷之中共浮沉,在床上缱绻终日。他俩还一起去了九州岛,在沙滩上追逐嬉笑,在岸上数着一浪接一浪的浪花,在峰顶的凉亭眺望一望无际的海洋,竹子的秀发和海风结成了朋友,临别依依,海风在船上抚弄她的秀发。

十二月二日晚,竹子想到明天一早就要走了,依依不舍,她说:"此后一别,不知何日再相逢?我要去了香港,我俩又要怎样才可团聚?"说着心一酸,就滚落了一串珠泪。

剑龙说:"总有办法解决的,我俩年轻,天大地大,任我俩大有作为。"

"兰姐说:故乡有许多人在办去纽西兰自费留学,这不失为一个好办法,你若先去了,我就容易跟随,不知你想不想去？"

"这确是一个好办法，我们机关里也有同事办，但要先辞去公职。我年轻，出去学好外语，练好本领应该还来得及发展，可我对搞留学之事知之不多。"

"这你不用担心，只要你想去，其他事我和兰姐帮手。"

"这事关系到我的事业去留，给我些时间考虑再决定。"

翌日一早，天还未亮就起了床，六点半的长途车，剑龙和竹子在宿舍里吻别，紧紧拥抱，仿佛别离是今生今世的事，剑龙备了灵芝乳鸽给兰姐，一袋苹果给坚儿，将一个镶有俩人合照的心形陀表给竹子戴上，秋风微冷，剑龙将外套披在竹子身上，风吹着她的飘动的秀发，泪水在她眶中打转，他说："不要哭，我俩总有办法早日团聚，不论是身在何处，永远为你祝福。"

她说："你要注意身体，多煮汤水喝！这次珠海行是我一生中最快乐的时光，谢谢你，亲爱的。"

"你使我成为一个最幸福的男人。"

要上车了，他俩紧紧相拥，竹子的泪滚落剑龙的肩上，她说："珍重。"

剑龙说："一路顺风！"

车子载着爱人绝尘而去，剑龙立于风中，直到车子消失在视野中……

竹子走了，房间一下子变得空洞，剑龙的心也是空荡荡的，若有所失，竹子的音容笑貌宛在，思念使人神思悠悠，魂魄也飞回了故乡。

这天吃过晚饭，同阿刚散完步回来，剑龙坐在桌前给竹子写信。

Bamboo missed the Jianlong and took a week's vacation. He

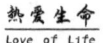
Love of Life

came to Zhuhai on November 27 to meet Ailang.

In the early morning of that day, the Jianlong got up early and went to the station to pick up bamboo. The lover is about to arrive, the Jianlong is excited, imagining the scene of the upcoming meeting, the autumn wind blowing, all turned into a warm spring. The car into the station, the window waving 1 hands–that's the bamboo the Jianlong is waiting!

When the bamboo got out of the car, the Jianlong stepped forward quickly, not afraid of embarrassment, and the two hugged tightly in the crowd! What evening is this evening, what year is this evening, how many hardships and twists have the men and women who love each other gone through before they meet again after a long time of parting? In the instant of the, tears came from the eyes of the bamboo, and the Jianlong also burst into tears. It was really mixed feelings and a long story.

"I'm so happy to finally have you here." said the Jianlong.

"I can't see your heart is not steadfast, hugging you feels so different!" Bamboo Road.

"Did you have a hard night's journey?" Jianlong pitied the hair of the bamboo geography.

"It's okay, just because I miss you all night!"

"Go back and take a hot bath first, rest your mind, and then go to drink tea. This the weekend, A Gang 1 class friends opened tea seats waiting for us."

Jianlong took the bamboo back to the dormitory. Jianlong lived alone in a suite with a small bed, but it could have space for two people to be alone. Bamboo was secretly happy and the big stone in his heart was put down, because he had been worried about his residence in Zhuhai, it would be inconvenient if he to be in the 1 room with other colleagues.

After taking a bath and changing into wide pajamas, Teresa Teng's song was on the indoor. The was singing "Sweet Honey" gently. The Jianlong was pruning and watering the flowers and plants. The bamboo looked at his focused expression. His heart was sweet,, soft, and comfortable. He kept the clouds open and the moon was bright. Should this be the state of mind? She gently closed her tired eyes.

Bamboo was very tired and slept until Agang called: "Jianlong, can you receive bamboo? Everyone is here, just waiting for you two, is it worth a thousand dollars at the moment of spring night?"

"Don't talk nonsense! When she arrived, she was very tired and asleep. You eat first, and we will be there in about half an hour."

After closing the thread, bamboo did not know when to get up, washed his face, put on lipstick, and had a fresh and moist breath on his cheeks, which made people shine at the moment –a beautiful woman!

Jianlong praised: "Bamboo you are very beautiful, natural beauty."

Bamboo smiled: "After a while of sleep, I feel better. How dare I meet people? When we meet for the first time, if there is an ugly man who scares his friends and loses your face, it will be miserable."

"There, such a beautiful girl and a gentleman are so charming that they have no time to praise ."

"Another flower, go quickly, or your brothers will be in a hurry."

At the restaurant of Yindu Hotel, it was already 11: 00 a.m. when everyone met 1, the opened. More than six feet high, A Gang, who was facing the wind in Yushu, stretched out his hand to hold the with the bamboo: "I am A Gang. Welcome to Zhuhai. Jianlong is really blessed and has made a woman like its name. Bamboo is just slender and elegant."

"A long long hair is tender like water, natural and unrestrained!" A Qiang said, looking back at his girlfriend Xia, who was cutting her short hair. A Xia laughed: "He seldom praises people. If he wants to say beauty, it is really beautiful. I like the bamboo pink dress very much, which just shows this delicate posture."

Jianlong smiled happily, and the bamboo was sweet in his heart. The fat Adong appeared somehow and inserted a 1 sentence: "I said bamboo has the best temperament, gentle and generous, and everyone loves it!"

1 heard him say "everyone loves everyone", everyone burst into laughter, saying that the fat boy was so brave that he couldn't help seeing a pretty girl. even his brother's girlfriend had a wild desire to. don't be anthomaniac in the future!

Adong is really in distress situation. Bamboo said: "Adong is just praising me. It is very difficult to develop a good temperament. I hope I deserve everyone's praise. Jianlong often mentions you to me. I am really very happy to meet you today. Please take care of me in the future."

Everyone shouted again before they started drinking tea.

Bamboo's response is generous and decent, and she has a good aura and. It seems that all her friends like her to join the circle.

Jianlong brothers are very honest and sincere, like a feather flock together, people are worthy of friends.

Not the kui is a peer, talk and smile during the dinner, time flies, all have enough to eat and drink, nearly 2 pm, a gang settled the account, proposed to go to the seaside park, everyone agreed, a line of people on the bus.

The road in Zhuhai is really wide. There is no problem six cars driving side by side. There are flowers and trees along the way. It is a veritable garden city in. Fresh air blows into the car and bamboo breathes happily. Everyone was talking and laughing. The car passed Jiuzhou Avenue, Zhuhai Hotel and Shijingshan and stopped in front of the seaside park.

There is a lush forest in the seaside park. Opposite Shijingshan beautiful with jagged rocks. The Milky White villas are dotted among the shadows of the trees. It like fairyland on earth. The 1 shower at noon will the of the mountain to look greener. After the rain, the clouds are floating cotton, drifting around the mountain.

When walking into the forest path, Gao Guang said, "I haven't been here for a long time. Look at these trees, the taller and denser they grow. I almost can't even find the road."

"brag, you have so many girlfriends who are dating all day long, even if you know every 1 grass here like the back of your hand." Feidong laughed at him.

"I am a rough person, where is so romantic? Jianlong is a famous gifted scholar in the organ. He is worthy of love in these green mountains and green waters. Now with bamboo, gifted scholars and beautiful women, it is really enviable!"

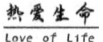
Love of Life

Everyone laughed, and Xia said, "Exactly, I don't have this blessing. A Qiang has never brought me to the park. I don't understand romance, alas."

"That's not what I said. A Qiang's cooking skills are recognized by everyone. It is much better to keep A Xia so beautiful than to visit the park." Jianlong way.

A Qiangxi said: "Jianlong is right. If you don't mind, please with Bamboo to Shea 1 sometime and try my side dishes. I don't chase beautiful women out of thin air."

"Hey, why don't you invite me and Ah Gang? The big is too, no, no!" Shouted adon.

"Of course, everyone will come and see how our two swords are combined!" Xia made a sword dance gesture in the air, and everyone laughed again.

Arriving in front of the statue of the fisherwoman in Zhuhai, the smiling fisherwoman stood in the middle of the sea, holding up the 1 pearl in her hands, holding up the joy of the Zhuhai people's hard work and harvest.

Everyone scattered. Jianlong and bamboo were sitting on a slightly damp reef. The light yellow sea water surged up wave by wave, slapping the reef and splashing strings of water. Some of them even hit them. In the autumn sun, the wind was cool and warm and blowing on their cheeks, lifting the hair of bamboo. A few white clouds were rolling in the sky. Some people were swimming in the sea. were floating in the water like fish, some children are flying kites on the shore.

Jianlong gently hugged the bamboo and listened to the low

singing of the sea tide. The mood was rare and relaxed. The bamboo said, "Your friends are so nice, affectionate and righteous, funny and humorous. It's really nice to be with them."

"We have been friends for almost ten years. We have grown up together and understood each other. We really have deep feelings. If we leave them in the future, we will be reluctant to part with them."

"I understand that it's just a feast that comes to an end in life. Some things should be let go when they should be let go, and those who are predestined friends will meet again one day."

Seeing Jianlong a little sad, Bamboo said, "Ah Gang appreciates you very much. People are also very generous. You and he can be described as swordsmen poetic hearts."

"I have the best relationship with him, and I am closer than my brother. Although he is tall and strong, he actually has very careful, so his girlfriend is like a lantern, and he can't count it. I don't know which one is true." Jianlong way.

"Adon is very funny and humorous. Is he dating?"

"I didn't succeed in filming a few. I thought he was fat, and soon he broke up. In fact, he is very pure in heart, and he will know how cute he is when he gets along."

"A Qiang and A Xia are in good tune, and good have husband and wife."

"Yes, they are about to get married. A Qiang is the most sincere and practical person. He is the most sure of the things entrusted to him. He is a friend worthy of long-term friendship. As for Xia, she is generous and decent, funny and humorous, and the two are really a good match."

Talking, unconsciously the sunset glow has drifted away in the western sky, the leaves are trembling, and they are walking the heat of the day. Also, after making a big umbrella for the shade of the day, beautifying the garden and cooling the tourists, it is time to stretch out their tired muscles and bones. After the 1 night, they have to repeat the same work. A little bit of home sail back to with sunset ...

"The scenery at dusk is really beautiful! The setting sun is infinitely good." Bamboo said.

"Soon it will be at the willow tip on the moon, and it will be after dusk," Jianlong suggested, "Do you want to go to the seaside?"

"Good!"

Then, the bamboo took the arm of the Jianlong and walked along the coast, the sea breeze. In the evening breeze, the sound of waves beating the shore became more and more gentle. 1 flocks of seagulls were flying and playing on the shore, passing around the two. Gradually, they merged into the misty twilight on the beach.

The friends saw that they were still in high spirits, so they left and went back to the house first. The Jianlong and the Jianlong left line after line of footprints on the beach. They went straight to the sky to light up the moon and the stars all over the sky. When they were hungry, they went to the sea to the overseas Chinese hotel restaurant for dinner.

The Ganoderma lucidum pigeon here is the most famous. Pigeons are first mixed with Ganoderma lucidum flavored ingredients to well, then braised in soy sauce. The taste has penetrated into the meat the body. It is with orange juice. It is really a special dish made by secret and has endless aftertaste and efficacy. In addition, Dongjiang salt baked chicken and fresh fish,, Qian, onion and bean curd soup are also very good. It is also a 1 kind of enjoyment to 1 a dish of garlic cabbage, 1 a pot of longevity hot tea, and sit on the dining table looking at the sea near the window.

The two of them were hungry, and the food was served at one end.

Jianlong asked: "How does the dish taste?"

"Taste well, this ganoderma lucidum pigeon, let my teeth and cheeks stay fragrant, memorable."

"So I call this dish every time I come, and everyone is delicious."

"Do you have any takeout? I want to take two back to Lanjie to try."

"There must be. Let me arrange it."

After dinner, walk along the long Jingshan Road. The road, which is almost 10 o'clock, is sparsely populated and the night is very quiet. The autumn sky is high,, cool and. The air is fresh and makes people breathe very freely. The night wind was a little cold. Bamboo brought her body close to Jianlong, showing infinite tenderness between her eyebrows. She said, "Dragon, I am really happy and comfortable today. Thank you and your friends."

"I haven't been so happy for a long time. You bring us joy."

"Lovers, friends, wonderful scenery, delicious food, life can be spent like this, is also a 1 kind of luck."

...

Back to the dormitory, took a bath, it was already midnight, late at night, most people have fallen asleep, the night is as cool as water, the surroundings seem so quiet and quiet.

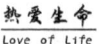

Jianlong played a romantic song of lovers, "Love Story" a song sounded gently in the ear, haunting in the heart, bamboo lying on the bed, his face blush, star eyes blurred, Jianlong turned off the overhead lamp, turned on the lamp, brought out the soft light, and then sat on the bed, looking at the bamboo affectionate: "The way you take a bath, like a pear out of clear water and a lotus, with a than the rain Yang."

After bathing together, I went back to bed, my body and mind were indescribable, and every cell in my body was telling love.

Bamboo said: "It's really wonderful, the pleasure is like a fairyland, the shrinking 1 brake has become eternal!"

"So this is the highest level of the combination of spirit and flesh." Jianlong way.

"Women have this baby, how can men resist?"

"That's why there are such beautiful ladies and gentlemen."

"No wonder men are so horny."

"I didn't expect you to be so strong as a scholar."

The bamboo pillow was on the arm of the Jianlong, and fell asleep while talking. the Jianlong looked at her rose-colored cheeks and satisfied face, smelled the faint fragrance scattered from her hair, and soon sank into the dreamland. the night was and gentle. the moonlight shone into the window and quietly sprinkled on the lovers, and couldn't help giving a knowing smile...

When dawn broke in the East, the bamboo woke up in the smile of the Jianlong, and the dreamless sweet sleep made her more and more delicate and charming. The woman in love is the most beautiful. At the moment, she deeply felt it. She looked at the Jianlong affectionately and her heart was full of happiness.

For the next six days, there was no difference between the morning and the night. They both floated and sank in the peaks and valleys of lust and stayed in bed all day long. They also went to the Kyushu Island together, chasing and laughing on the beach, counting waves after waves on the shore, and looking out at the endless ocean from the pavilion on the summit. The bamboo hair and the sea breeze became friends. After parting, the sea breeze stroked her hair on the boat.

On the evening of December 2, bamboo thought that she would leave early tomorrow morning and was reluctant to part with her. she said, "after a farewell, I don't know when we will meet again? I'm going to Hong Kong, how can we be reunited? "Saying a sad heart, rolling down the 1 beads of tears.

Jianlong said: "There is always a way to solve it. We are young and big, so we can do a lot."

"Sister Lan said: There are many people in my hometown who run in to New Zealand study abroad at their own expense. This is a good way. If you go first, I will easily follow. I wonder if you want to go?"

"This is indeed a good way, our organs also have colleagues to run, but first to resign from public office. I am young and. I go out to learn a foreign language well. I should still have time to develop my skills, but I don't know much about study abroad."

"You don't have to worry about this. As long as you want to go, Lan Jie and I will help you with other things."

"This matter is related to my career. Give me some time to consider before deciding."

热爱生命
Love of Life

The next morning, I got up before dawn. At 6:30, the long-distance bus, Jianlong and bamboo kissed goodbye and hugged tightly in the dormitory, as if parting was a matter of this life. Jianlong prepared Ganoderma lucidum pigeon for Lanjie, 1 a bag of apples for Jian, a heart-shaped tuo watch with two people taking pictures to wear on bamboo. The autumn wind was slightly cold and Jianlong drapo, the wind was blowing her fluttering hair, and tears were swirling in the of her eyes. He said, "Don't cry, there is always a way for us to get together as soon as possible. No matter where we are, we will always bless you."

She said: "You should pay attention to your health and more soup to drink! This trip to Zhuhai is the happiest time in my life. Thank you, dear."

"You make me the happiest man."

As they were about to get on the bus, they hugged each other tightly. Bamboo tears rolled down Jianlong's shoulders. She said, "Take care."

Jianlong said, "Bon voyage!"

The car carried his lover away, and the Jianlong stood in the wind until the car disappeared from view ...

When the bamboo is gone, the room suddenly becomes empty, and the heart of the sword dragon is also empty. If something is lost, the sound, appearance and smile of the bamboo will be there. The missing makes people think leisurely and the soul will fly back to their hometown.

After dinner on this day, when he came back from a walk with Agang, Jianlong sat at the table and wrote to bamboo.

竹子：

一切可好？念你如痴，念你如诗！

11月27日－12月3日这7天7夜，时光飞一般过去，我俩的相逢和相处是那样动人心弦，销魂蚀骨，我们成了世界上最幸福的恋人。

别了才不过四日，恍如隔世。古人说一日不见如隔三秋，一点也不夸张。

身边没有你的音容笑貌，没有你的温柔缠绵，激荡豪情，没有你的关怀体贴，我心中若有所失。

入夜，微冷的宿舍，一室寂然。脑海中放映着我俩一起时的一幕幕生活，你的一言一笑，一举一动，都已一一植入了我的心间。我处于迷惑与清醒之间，原来男女的爱，到了灵与肉的结合，才真正明白什么是销魂蚀骨，什么是意乱情迷！

心中在喃喃自语：痴缠你，痴缠你，痴缠你。仿佛我仍在你的体内，那样的紧握，那样的拥抱，那样如胶似漆的缠绵，像水母一样的收缩和呼吸。

金风玉露一相逢，便胜却人间无数！

你编织的毛衣，丝丝缕缕都交织着爱意，我会好好珍藏。

凝视汽车将你载走，我狂追，直到它绝尘而去，留下我街上一个孤单的身影。家中这几日，你的音容宛在，但人已相隔越来越远，我的思念又乘机来袭，不知你一切可好？

何日君再来？

此后夜夜孤枕难眠，好想你呵，我的竹子，我温柔的妻。

永远爱你的夫郎，
剑龙
1989年12月7日

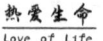

Bamboo:

Is everything okay? Read you like, read you like poetry!

From November 27 to December 3, this 7 days and 7 nights. Time flies by. Our meeting and getting along is so touching and fascinating. We have become the world's happiest lovers.

It's only been four days since I said goodbye. It's like a lifetime ago. The ancients said that one day is not as good as three autumn seasons, which is not an exaggeration at all.

Without your voice and smile, without your tenderness and touching, stirring lofty sentiments, without your care and consideration, if I have lost something in my heart.

At night, the slightly cold dormitory, the 1 room was silent. In my mind, I showed the scenes of our life together. Your words and smiles and every move have been implanted in my heart one by one. I am between confusion and sobriety. It turns out that the love between men and women has come to the combination of spirit and flesh before I really understand what is ecstasy and bone erosion and what is ecstasy!

Mumbling in the heart: infatuated with you, infatuated with you, infatuated with you. As if I am still in your body, so clenched, so hugged, so like glue lingering, like a jellyfish like contraction and breathing.

Gold wind jade dew 1 meet, then win the world countless!

The sweater you 've knitted is woven with love, and I'll treasure it.

Stare at the car to carry you away, I chase, until it is gone, leaving me a lonely figure on the street. In the past few days at home, your voice and appearance are there, but people are getting farther and farther apart, and my thoughts are coming again. I wonder if everything is okay with you?

When will you come again?

Since then, I have been lonely and sleepless every night. I miss you so much, my bamboo, my gentle wife.

Always love your husband,

Jianlong

7 December 1989

剑龙:

我的夫君!

刚离开你,人还在孤旅之中,思念之泪已溢满心湖。正是无情不似多情苦,一寸还成千万缕,相见时难别亦难呵。

才知道,情到深处人孤独,想你念你不肯像平日那样完全向兰姐诉说,一个人默默地在心中回味那份令人战栗,迷醉的温柔,泪——无端地浸在心头。

昨夜,窗外月色朦胧,我寒衣独拥,手中一部《唐宋词鉴赏辞典》伴我到天明。

今夜,铺开素笺,在灯下诉说我对你的思念,前尘往事,纷纷涌上心头。

7日销魂蚀骨的聚首,像黑夜里缥缈的幽灵,抚弄我的衣角,飞舞着诱惑和侵蚀我的思绪——今夕何夕?今夕何年?

夜正阑静,风正轻盈,我纤瘦的身影,微颤,无言。在灯下细细梳理记忆,不禁喜极而泣,扪心自问:此生何幸?能独享你风情万种的情爱?此生何幸,得以在你跟前恣意舒展!

7日的时光,你令我长成了一位风情万种的女子,二十几年的积累，在7日里得到了升华，二十几年的委屈，在你轻言软语之中烟消云散，知否？你的深爱，是我作为一个女子毕生的殊荣和幸福，毕生的骄傲和自豪！我昏睡的情感，由于你真诚的启拨，徐徐苏醒，以至汹涌不绝，是你，令我成为一个柔情万斛的女人。

爱你，我的夫郎，死心塌地，长醉不醒！

从别后，忆相逢，几回梦魂与君同，今宵剩把银缸照，犹恐相逢在梦中。

7日的如怨如慕，如幻如真，秦观一句：金风玉露一相逢，便胜却人间无数！素笺寸管，难以表达我对你的爱慕、敬重、痴迷、思念和不舍，也述不了灵肉结合之后那份渴求、温柔、缠绵与美妙，那如常春藤一般的生死相缠！真正的幸福竟然是一片迷乱，和战栗的空茫，像天与地，象落霞与孤鹜，如高山流水，契合得不着痕迹，既有前无古人的苍凉，亦有蓦然回首，那人却在灯火阑珊处的泪流。

月朗风清之夜，我挽你的手，在星月交辉的天穹之下漫步，时而私语，时而相顾大笑，划破了夜的温柔，是那样浪漫，那样温馨，你，是我心里梦里的情人。

人生代代无穷已，江畔年年月相似，相似的是这个古老而永恒的主题，让我俩以现代的风貌，觅骨子血脉里古典的情怀，踏入唐诗宋词的境界，或浓墨重彩，或高亢长啸，或低吟浅唱，或飘逸风流，缠绵轻愁。

我俩随意而写，或是踏着如水的调子相偎相拥，如风抚杨柳，柳絮迎风，我俩歌如云雀，拥着烈焰，轻翔歌唱或歌唱轻翔，或者，如疯狂的水兵，合著骤雨的曲子，滑进平川绿野，又跃上峻岭山岩……

我俩每天玩着过家家的游戏，淡泊得如阳春白雪，又在朋友之中高谈阔论，且心地留白，凝视刹那，那种偷偷的感觉，令人心跳脸红，不能言语，真是妙不可言！

聪敏与痴迷皆由君牵引，琴音的劣拙或美妙都赖君的巧手。弹奏如仙乐，不禁惊叹君的高妙，纵然就此一生，亦了无遗憾。我愿长久地，在日后，永为你温柔聪慧的妻，敬你，爱你，鼓励你，信任你一生！窗外，一弯月儿天如水，我俩从俗又脱俗的心性，如这明净的月，世上许多事，漏过了，在我俩心里只有美丽，无论将来日子清贫或富贵，相信都会过得一样的香醇。想你时，心有千言万语，涌着万点柔情。

我的妙人儿呵，离情正引千丝乱！

夫君晚安，伴我入梦，好想你哦……

痴爱你的竹妻
1989年12月7日，故乡。

Jianlong:

My husband!

Just left you, people are still in the of a lonely journey, the tears of missing have filled the heart lake. It is ruthlessness that is not like affectionate bitterness. One inch is still inextricably linked. It is also difficult to say goodbye when we meet.

Only then did I know that people are lonely in the depths of love. I miss you that you are not willing to tell Lanjie completely as usually do. A person silently recalled the chilling, intoxicating tenderness and tears in his heart–unprovoked.

Last night, the moonlight outside the window was dim, I my cold clothes and holding alone. I had a Dictionary of Appreciation of Tang and Song Ci with me until dawn.

Tonight, I spread out my notes and tell my missing for you under the lamp. The past has poured into my heart.

The gathering of the 7th, like ethereal ghosts in the of the night, fondling my clothes, dancing with temptation and eroding my thoughts–what evening is this evening? What year is this evening?

Night is quiet, wind is light, I slim figure, trembling, speechless. Under the lamp carefully combing the memory, can not help but cry with joy, ask yourself: this life how lucky? Can you enjoy the love of your? He is lucky to be in this life, and can and stretch in front of you!

On the 7th, you made me grow into a 1 woman with a lot of style. After more than 20 years of accumulation, I was sublimated on the 7th. More than 20 years of grievances disappeared in your soft words. Know? Your deep love is my lifelong honor and happiness as a woman, my lifelong pride and pride! My lethargic emotion, due to your sincere enlightenment and, woke up slowly and even surged endlessly. It was you who made me a tender woman.

Love you, my husband, lang, dead set, long drunk!

After parting, I remember meeting each other. I dreamed of being with you several times. I took the silver jar this night. I was afraid of meeting in my dream.

On the 7th, resentment was like admiration, like fantasy, Qin Guan said: if the golden wind and jade dew meet 1, they will win the world countless! It is difficult to express my love, respect, obsession, missing and not giving up for you. I can't the thirst, tenderness, touching and beauty after the combination of spirit and flesh in the., the life and death like Ivy! The real happiness turned out to be a confusion, and the emptiness the trembling of the, is like the sky and the ground, like the sunset and the lonely of the, such as high mountains and flowing water, fit without trace, both unprecedented desolation, there are suddenly looking back, but the man in the dim lights of the tears.

On a clear and windy night, I took your hand and strolled under the sky of stars and moon, sometimes whispering and laughing, breaking the tenderness of the night. It was so romantic and warm. You were the lover in my dream.

The generations of life are endless, and the years and months on the riverside are similar. What is similar is this ancient and eternal theme, which makes us step into the realm of Tang and Song poetry with modern style, looking for classical feelings in bones and blood, either with thick ink and heavy color, or high-pitched roaring, or low-pitched and shallow singing, or elegant and romantic, lingering sad and.

We write at will, or cuddle with each other in a water-like tone, like the wind caressing willows, willow catkins facing the wind, we singing like lark, holding the flames, singing or singing, or, like crazy sailors, singing together with the song of showers, sliding into Pingchuan green fields, and leaping up mountains and rocks...

We play the game of playing house every day. We are as indifferent as spring and white snow. We talk loudly among our friends. and, we the white and stare at the instant of the. The feeling of secretly makes our hearts blush and can't speak. It's really wonderful!

Cleverness and obsession are all drawn by the of Jun. The and inferiority of the piano sound or wonderful Lai Jun's skillful hands. Playing such as fairy music, can not help but marvel at your wonderful, even in this life, also no regrets. I would like to long-term, in the future, for your gentle and intelligent wife, respect and you, love you, encourage you, trust you for a lifetime! Outside the window, the moon is like water, and our vulgar and refined mind, such as this clear and clean month, has missed many things in the world. In our hearts, there is only beauty. No matter whether we are poor or rich in the future, we believe we will live the same mellow life. When I miss you, my heart has a thousand words and a thousand tenderness.

My wonderful person, the departure is leading thousands of silk chaos!

Good night husband, accompany me to dream, miss you so much...

Love your bamboo wife

December 7, 1989, home.

竹子：

从别后，忆相逢，几回梦魂与君同，今宵剩把银缸照，犹恐相逢在梦中。

想你在时间之内，想你在时间之外，想你成纵横交错的相思。

你是神灵飘绕在我的舍内，在洒满甘霖的青枝绿叶上，你飘浮在远方的云端，那如幻似真的七天七夜，仿佛天方夜谭，更似鬼怪妖魔挥动的魔棒，我俩已经沉溺，沉醉不解东风。

11月27日－12月3日这7天，时光如飞，永恒的已活在记忆。

仍清楚记得你坐车由故乡来赴约的夜晚，我兴奋得一盏孤灯伴到天明。那心里梦里的风景，莫道不销魂。

你的情笺散在我的桌子枕畔，随手抽出来阅读，你的痴心是一瓣瓣醉人的情英，艳丽，痴迷，执着，凛冽。

邓丽君的：我只在乎你，轻轻萦绕耳畔，心温柔光滑得如一缎锦。

夜色伴思念醉成酒红色。

天色未明，就带上锁出门等你，心中是快乐舒畅的歌调。

一辆辆车来了又开走了，怎么不见我心里梦里的爱人？

直到太阳帅哥点燃黎明，一辆故乡开来的大巴上，终于跳出了你欢跃开心的身影，我俩在晨光熹微的车站，紧紧地拥抱在一起，我热烈的吻，印在你疲惫迷人的发端，今夕何夕？古月头上照新人。

拿起行李，手牵着手回我的宿舍，你坐在那张肥婆椅上，伴着曙色，执手相看泪眼，忽然你泪如雨下，我以唇，吻干你的泪痕。

我们这一对冤家，在叶落尽的秋天，再一次相聚，这次，我们终于紧紧地拥抱在一起，仿佛天地在此刻，已然终止。

七天，我俩牵手，快乐地走在珠海的大街小巷。我骄傲地把你介绍给机关里的一班好友。强和霞夫妇微笑看着我们，高佬刚开心地坐在肥婆椅上喝未来嫂子用电饭煲煮的鸡汤，肥东一如平常，笑成弥勒佛的贝齿闪闪发光，华与周，坚与芬夫妇也高兴迎接我俩，我们在好友相聚中大口喝茶，在举杯痛饮中大块吃肉，谈笑风生，我们在老友善意调侃的眼光中心跳耳热，偷吃禁果的感觉在脸上发烧，我们在彼此目光中秘密交流，配合默契，喜悦在空气中曼妙多姿，妙不可言，还有什么比和好友分享和完全接受我们的爱情，更令人心旷神怡？

七天七夜，天堂里的日子，我俩长成了一对璧人，你的风情万种，在我密集的鼓点中，驰骋千里，跃马原野，又在我们温柔的缠绵中，如胶似漆，难舍难分。

我俩一如夫妇，手牵手去菜市场讨价还价，抱回我们的战利品，由你的巧手负责变出美味佳肴，我一顿饭喝你七碗汤豪举，在我俩大汗淋漓的巫山云雨中歌舞翩跹。

珠海的浪漫的沙滩，宽敞美丽的马路，都留下了我们春风欢畅的身影，跑遍大街小巷撑台脚，做一对如假包换的吃货，快乐是我们笑得见牙而不见了眼睛。

七天七夜，飞一般过去，再回首，你已经远走，没有你的宿舍，顷刻间了无生趣，寂寞乘机来袭，恍若隔世。

身边没有你的音容笑貌，温馨软语，没有你的狡黠灵慧，没有你的温柔缠绵，激荡昂扬，没有你秘密花园的芳香醉人，没有你常春藤般的痴痴缠缠，我若有所失。

夜，微冷的宿舍，我寂然，脑中放映一幕幕缠绵的情景，你的一言一笑，一举一动，都已一一植入我的心灵深处。

我处于迷惑清醒之间，原来男女的情爱，唯有到了灵与肉的结合，那样忘我投入的生死交流，才真正明白：什么是销魂蚀骨？什么叫意乱情迷。

眼神迷离飘忽，心中喃喃自语：竹子我的亲亲，我要痴缠你、痴缠你、痴缠你。

仿佛我仍在你芬芳的花园，那样的拥抱，那样的迷醉，那样如胶似漆的缠绵。

7日7夜，分不清晨昏昼夜，情欲的分享这般动人，原始的欲望那样令人不可息止，涌起时如熊熊烈火，沉静下去便柔情万千，枕畔书香阵阵，你如兰的呼吸，宁如婴孩的睡容，都太美妙动人，那种欲仙欲死的感觉，羽化而仙登。

原来，你二十六岁的寻寻觅觅，我二十多岁生命的苦苦追寻，都是为了在这俊美的华年，在这美丽如诗的一刻，紧紧相拥，灵肉相牵相引相缠，我俩终于合而为一了，落霞与孤鹜齐飞,秋水共长天一色,从此,再没有什么外力可以将我俩分开。

金风玉露一相逢,便胜却人间无数。

亲爱的妙人儿噢,你亲手为我织成的墨绿色毛衣,丝丝缕缕交织着爱的深意,我今夜把它披在身上,暖透身心,这份美丽动人的情意,我必珍藏一生。

凝望汽车再次把你载走,我狂追,直到你消失于我的视野,留下我街中孤零零一个寂寞无依的身影。

转眼间,人已阻隔万水千山,夜的足音轻轻响起,我的思念乘机来袭,雁过也,正伤心,却是旧时相识!

夜风中走在拱北宾馆海边,默数你孤单的归程,我的竹子哦,不知你旅途可顺畅安宁?

是否你也如我这般,心里梦里,又纵横写满了相思。

相见时难别亦难,东风无力百花残,一日如隔三秋的思绪,眉间心头,无计消除。

好想你噢,白日依山尽,长河落日圆,何日君再来,更尽一杯酒?

天长地久有时尽,此情绵绵无绝期。

我的竹子,我温柔的妻。

念你的夫郎
剑龙
12月8日,珠海

Bamboo:

After paring, I remember meeting each other. I dreamed of being with you several times. I took the silver jar this night. I was afraid of meeting in my dream.

Think of you in time, think of you in time, think of you into a

Love of Life

crisscross acacia.

You are a god floating around my house, on green branches and green leaves sprinkled with showers, you float in the clouds in the distance, it is like a real seven days and seven nights, like a fantasy, more like a magic wand waved by ghosts and demons, we have been addicted, intoxicated and puzzled by the east wind.

From November 27 to December 3, this 7 days, time flies, and eternity has lived in memory.

I still clearly remember the night when you came to the appointment by car from my hometown. I was so excited that I was accompanied by a lonely lamp to till dawn. The scenery in the dream of the heart, Mo Tao is not ecstasy.

Your love scattered on my desk pillow, casually pulled out to read, your infatuation is a piece of intoxicating love English, gorgeous, infatuated, persistent, bitter.

Teresa Teng's: I only care about you, gently lingering in my ears, my heart is as gentle and smooth as satin brocade.

Night with miss drunk into wine red.

Before the sky is clear, I will take the lock and go out to wait for you. My heart is full of happy and comfortable tunes.

Cars came and drove away. Why didn't I see my lover in my dream?

Until the handsome boy in the sun lit the dawn, 1 a bus from his hometown, finally jumped out of your happy figure. We hugged each other tightly at the station in the early morning light. My warm kiss was printed on your tired and charming hair end. What evening is this evening? Gu Yue's head a new person.

剑龙与竹子的情书，惊艳了岁月
Jianlong and bamboo love letter, amazing years

Pick up the luggage, hand in hand back to my dormitory, you sit in the fat woman chair, accompanied by dawn, holding hands to look at the tears, suddenly your tears, I with lips, kiss dry your tears.

We this pair of enemies, in the fall of the leaves, once again together, this time, we finally hugged tightly together, as if heaven and earth at this moment, has ended.

For seven days, we walked happily in the streets of Zhuhai hand in hand. I am proud to introduce you to my 1 class friends in the machine. Qiang and Xia and his wife looked at us with a smile. Gao Lao just happily sat on the chair of fat woman and to drink chicken soup cooked by future sister-in-law with an electric rice cooker. Feidong was as usual. smiled and into Maitreya's teeth shining. Hua and Zhou, Jian and and wife were also happy to welcome us. We drank tea with a big cup and drank meat with a big smile, in the center of the eyes of our old friends who are kind and ridiculed, our ears are hot, and the feeling of stealing forbidden fruits is feverish on our faces. We communicate secretly in each other's eyes, cooperate with each other, and our joy is wonderful and wonderful in the air. What is more refreshing than sharing and fully accepting our love with our friends?

Seven days and seven nights, the days in heaven, we have grown into a pair of lovers. You have a thousand kinds of customs. In my dense drumbeat, you gallop thousands of miles, leap over the wilderness, and in our gentle lingering, like glue, hard to part.

Like a couple, we went to the vegetable market hand in hand to bargain, took back our spoils of war, and your skillful hands were responsible for making delicious food. I drink seven bowls of soup for a meal, singing and dancing in the clouds and rain of Wushan, where

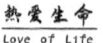

we were sweating profusely.

The romantic beaches and spacious and beautiful roads in Zhuhai have left us with a happy figure in the spring breeze. We have run all over the streets and alleys to support our feet and make a pair of fake food. Happiness is that we can see our teeth and without eyes.

Seven days and seven nights, flying past, and then looking back, you have gone far away, without your dormitory, instantly boring, lonely opportunity to attack, as if a lifetime.

Without your voice, smile, warm and soft words, without your cunning spirit, without your tenderness, touching and stirring, without the fragrance and intoxicating of your secret garden, without your ivy-like infatuation, if I have lost anything.

At night, in the slightly cold dormitory, I was silent, and scenes of lingering scenes were shown in my mind. Your words and smiles and every move have been implanted in my heart one by one.

I am between confused and awake, the original love between men and women, only to the combination of spirit and flesh, so selfless into the exchange of life and death, can really understand: what is the soul eroded bone? What do you mean, crazy.

My eyes blurred and drifted, and my heart muttered to myself: Bamboo, my kiss, I want to pester you, I want to pester you, I want to pester you.

As if I am still in your fragrant garden, so embrace, so intoxicated, so lingering like glue.

On the 7th and 7th nights, I can't tell the difference between the morning and the night. The sharing of lust is so moving. The original desire is so unstoppable. When it gushes up, it is like a raging fire.

When it is quiet, it will be tender and tender. The fragrance of books beside the pillow. Your breathing like orchid and the sleeping capacity of like a baby are all too wonderful and moving. The feeling of dying immortals is feathered and.

It turns out that your search at the age of 26 and my hard search for life in my twenties are all for years in this beautiful China. At this beautiful poetic moment, we hugged each other tightly, led by spirit and flesh, led by and entangled. We finally became one. Sunset and Lone Harrier Qi Fei, autumn waters shared the same color. From then on, no external force could separate us.

When the golden wind and jade dew meet 1, they win the world countless.

Dear wonderful person, the dark green sweater you woven for me with your own hands is intertwined with the deep meaning of love. I put it on my body tonight to warm my body and mind. I will treasure this beautiful and moving affection for my whole life.

Gazing at the car to carry you away again, I chased you wildly until you disappeared from my sight, leaving a lonely figure in my street.

In a twinkling of an eye, people have blocked thousands of rivers and mountains, the night's footnotes ring gently, my thoughts take the opportunity to attack, wild goose also, is sad, but it is an old acquaintance!

Walking on the seaside of Gongbei Hotel in the night wind, counting your lonely return journey. My bamboo, I wonder if your journey can be smooth and peaceful?

Whether you are like me, the dream in my heart is full of acacia.

When we meet each other, it is difficult to say no, the east wind is

热爱生命
Love of Life

weak and all flowers are residual. One day is like the thoughts of three autumns, the brow in the heart, and there is no to eliminate.

I miss you so much. The white sun is over the mountains, the long river is setting and the sun is setting. When will you come again, and 1 a glass of wine?

The days and the days are long and the days are long and the days are endless.

My bamboo, my gentle wife.

Miss your husband lang

Jianlong

December 8, Zhuhai

后记

有情人终成眷属，剑龙和竹子终于冲破一切阻力成为夫妇，竹子首先赴港定居，剑龙辞去公务员一职，办理自费留学受阻，经历四年漫长的等待和两地分离的刻骨煎熬，终于得以赴港夫妻团聚，本以为一切由此转好，谁知更残酷的考验从天而降，香港现实冷酷，一切从头开始，要成功突围逆袭，谈何容易，更何况人生无常，天意弄人，到头来，花谢花飞飞满天。

岁月漏过指尖，忧伤又马不停蹄，春花秋月何时了，往事知多少，小楼昨夜又东风，故情不堪回首月明中。

碧云天，黄叶地，今宵月色应如水，问君能有几多愁，恰似一江春水向东流。

剑龙终于读完以上章节，他长叹一声，把笔记翻到首页，那里有这样一段独白：

竹子我爱，我已将我俩爱的悲欢离合记在这里，无论幸与不幸，这都是我俩生命一段最忠实诚挚的记忆，在万千同类中，爱情能有我俩境界和经历的，微乎其微，我曾经希望能长燃对你的恋火，借此燃亮你的一生。

诚然，我俩都曾不顾一切焚身以火，擦亮彼此的生命，即便今天我俩已渐行渐远，但我对自己当初的选择无怨无悔，我俩如此呕心沥血为爱痴狂，才成就了这段刻骨铭心的爱恋，我感激你丰荣了我的生命，感激上苍让我俩同台共演这一场爱的悲欢离合。

一场生死决绝的大病，让我大半年生不如死，令你忧心如焚，悔不当初，愁肠百结，与其在绝望中捆绑着你沉沦，我宁愿独自饮下这杯毒酒，放爱人一条生路，就这样在大病有点起色的时候，我决定离开你，就算死也让我独自一个人死在外面，我既然已经不能带给你幸福，那么就让我独自忍耐这份别离的痛楚，只要你今后能够过上健康快乐的日子，你的幸福就是剑龙的快乐，再苦再累我也要给你一个开心的笑容。于是，我在你出差的日子，没有留下片言只语，悄然离家出走，走向茫茫孤单的未知，风雨飘摇，举目无亲，我但求独自挣扎求存，也不愿给你和亲人增添痛苦与烦忧。

就这样分开了，在彼此生命最迷惘最脆弱的时辰，我甚至没来得及恢复精神与清醒，于分手前给你一个解释，我走后听说你认定我已移情别恋，痛彻心扉，再后来又听说你嫁了北欧一位洋牧师，生活得快乐幸福，我衷心为你高兴为你祝福，你若与他幸福快乐生活下去，我即便独自在海角天涯漂泊到老，即便你永远也不知道我离开你的真相，就此一生，亦了无遗憾。

情路上不说谁对谁错，在一起彼此能否兼容，相处是否愉快、合适，能不能共同面对困境、理解包容、不离不弃，一起过好油盐柴米平淡深远的日子，才是生活的关键，人生，永远是一个走着取舍的过程。

时光太匆促，和谐之乐去得太快，对于将来，我所求的不过是一种淡泊宁静，平淡深远，健康和乐的日子。

真爱，美丽如诗，丰沛如泉，真情挚爱，诗情画意，悲欢交织，是不能忘记的，真爱的故事必将刻骨铭心，地老天荒，永恒不灭！

　　读到这里，剑龙轻轻合上这两本爱的笔记，他疾步走出中环广场，走向渡头，其时秋空辽阔夜色深浓，他登上轮渡，任海风吹拂黑发，启航的笛音划破夜空，他的身影，终于融进维多利亚港霭霭暮色中。

Postscript

　　When lovers finally got married, Jianlong and bamboo finally broke through all resistance and became a couple. Bamboo first settled in Hong Kong. Jianlong resigned as a civil servant and was blocked from studying abroad at his own expense. After four years of long waiting and the bitter suffering of separation between the two places, he was finally able to reunite with the couple in Hong Kong. I thought everything would turn for the better, but the more cruel test came from heaven. Hong Kong's reality was cold, in the end, flowers are flying all over the sky.

　　The years missed fingertips, sadness and non-stop, when is the spring flower and autumn moon, how much do you know about the past, the small building last night and the east wind, so can't bear to look back on the moon.

　　Blue sky, yellow leaves, this night moon color should be like

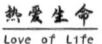
Love of Life

water, ask you can have how much sorrow, just like a river spring water flowing eastward.

Jianlong finally finished reading the above chapters. He sighed 1 and turned his notes to the front page. There was a monologue like this:

Bamboo I love, I have already remembered the joys and sorrows of our love here. Whether lucky or unfortunate, this is the most faithful and sincere memory of our life. Among thousands of similar people, love can have our realm and experience, which is very small. I once hoped to burn's love for you for a long, take this to brighten your life.

It is true that both of us have made great efforts to burn ourselves to the fire and polish each other's lives. Even though we are drifting away today, I have no regrets about my original choice. We are so crazy about love that we have achieved this unforgettable love. I am grateful that you have my life and that God has let us play the joys and sorrows of 1 love together.

1 is a serious illness that has made me worse than death for more than half a year. It worries you, repents you, and worries you. Instead of binding you to sink in despair, I would rather drink this poisoned wine alone let love a way out. In this way, when the serious illness is a little better, I decided to leave you. Even if I die, I will die alone. Since I can't bring you happiness, then let me endure the pain of separation alone. As long as you can live a healthy and happy life in the future, your happiness is the happiness of Jianlong. No matter how hard and tired I am, I will give you a happy smile. Therefore, on the day of your business trip, I did not leave a single word. I quietly ran away from home and went to the boundless and lonely unknown. I only wanted to

struggle for survival alone, and I did not want to add pain and worry to you and your relatives.

I separated in this way. I didn't even have time to recover my spirit and sober up in the most confused and vulnerable time of each other's lives. I gave you an explanation before I broke up. After I left, I heard that you decided that I had changed my love and felt very sad. Later, I heard that you married 1 foreign priest in Northern Europe and lived happily. I sincerely wish you happiness. If you live happily with him, even if I am alone in the ends of the earth wandering to the old, even if you never know the truth that I left you, this life, also no regrets.

The key to life is not to say who is right and who is wrong, whether we can be compatible with each other, whether we can get along happily and appropriately, whether we can face difficulties together, understand and tolerate, never give up, and live a plain and far-reaching life together. Life is always a process of choice.

Time is too hasty, the joy of harmony goes too fast, and for the future, all I want is to 1 a quiet, dull, healthy and happy day.

True love, beautiful as poetry, abundant as springs, true love, poetic and picturesque, joys and sorrows intertwined, can not be forgotten, the story of true love will be engraved on the heart, the end of the world, eternal!

After reading this, Jianlong gently closed these two love notes. He walked quickly out of the Central Square and walked to the ferry. At that time, the autumn was vast and the night was dark. He boarded the ferry and let the sea breeze blow his black hair. The sound of the flute set sail cut through the night sky. His figure finally melted into the mist and dusk of Victoria Harbour.

一个抑郁症患者的手记

Notes of a depressed patient

前言

我叫笔子,我不幸患上了严重的抑郁症,我的身体和生活一切都变得面目全非了。

整天头脑昏沉沉的,似睡非睡,无时无刻产生的焦虑与不安,令人痛不欲生。

吃药已经成了习惯,大把大把的药吞进肚里,就是为了一天过得安宁和平和。

杜珞斯丁,是主要的抗抑郁症的药,我现在每天吃150mg,再加上奥氮平和兰密顿,这都是我每天必上的功课,药一点也不能少。

患病的日子,每天都很难度过。

我定不了神看书和看电视,写字也是今天:2019年12月22日星期日,才重新开始尝试,希望由此再重拾旧欢,以此填补我大把大把的空余时间。也赶走脑子里时不时出现的胡思乱想和软弱无力。

医生说,我会慢慢好起来的,我需要耐心和坚持,同时保持锻炼身体。每当我感觉不错的时候,我相信她的话,但是当我感觉不舒服,脑子和身体都不听使唤的时候,我就变得比较悲观。

我现在每天大多数时间都在睡觉或者尝试睡觉,因为唯有睡觉令我觉得时间比较容易度过,一睡解千愁,在没有找到其他好办法的时候,我还是会在睡眠中一天天度过。

今天写下这些文字，使我感觉我的思维还是有条理的清晰的，这给我很大的信心和鼓励，用这个方法我还是比较轻易就能填满闲暇的时光。

我相信能够写上一页，就能写上十页和更多的文字。

被抑郁控制了脑子思想和身体行动的感受是极其痛苦的，没有经过这种折磨的人，是难以想象其症状的，许多人至今还认为这不过就是心中一点忧郁的情绪而已，只要放宽心情，一切看开了，病情也就好了。如果抑郁症如这些人所想，那么就没有那么多患者不得不选择了自尽来结束生命与痛苦，我现在才感同身受，非常明白这些人的选择是迫于无奈的，可以理解。

自从去年九月以来，我被抑郁症折磨得死去活来，很长时间像行尸走肉一样活着，也多次想过轻生，得以解脱，但尼尔如果没有了我，一个人在凯恩斯一定会孤单寂寞，我不忍一个人先走，活下去，能陪伴多久就多久吧。

现在我每天傍晚都和尼尔一起去海边散步，每次散完步回家，微微出汗，心情也轻松愉快，人确实需要运动或走动一下，活络筋骨，呼吸新鲜空气，加强血液循环，毕竟对身体是好的。

回想，我的抑郁症是因为长期失眠而起的，长期失眠的滋味真不好受，我至今也没有找到很好的药物改善自己的睡眠。但有一种叫 Sleep EZY 的草本植物胶囊，对我夜晚的睡眠有些帮助，也没有什么不好的副作用。

我很久都没有更新我们的微信公众号平台了，因为抑郁症的反反复复，令我不得不暂时放弃了平台的发展，精神不济，少了对平台的维护，自然也少了不少生活的交流与乐趣。

我今天能够写下上面这些文字，证明我的身体状况有了改善，我要好好享受此刻的来之不易，争取把自己的经历和思想记录下来，让读者对抑郁症有更深入的了解，也更理解患者的痛苦和不易。

对于患者，家人的理解是很重要的，因为患者的许多体验和状况看起来都是不可思议的，好比：患者往往因为看不到任何生存的希望而对生活失去了信心。患者会被病魔控制和剥夺了求生能力，使其思想和身体瘫痪，不能思想和行动，失去生活的力量。此外抑郁症也会由多方面打击患者的信心和勇气，促使病人着手结束自己的生命。

患者的身体检查许多时候都是正常的，但问题出现在精神上，而病情也分心因性和身体功能性的，心因性患病的例子很多，比如情感失控，环境大变换，突发的事件等等，而我的病情是属于神经功能的衰弱，引起失眠，然后由长期失眠导致抑郁症。

抗抑郁药物的副作用也不少。便秘是其中一个。所以我们在家里常备通便的药物和食物，平时注意多喝水。还有就是药物会引起低血压，站起来常常会感到头晕眼花，过一会才恢复正常。

患者每天都要和病魔搏斗，不能被病魔完全控制了思想和行动，有机会就要让自己反过来掌握和控制，给自己信心和勇气，相信医生和药物会帮助自己恢复健康和带给自己快乐。

每天按时按量服用抗抑郁的药，遇到焦虑不安的时候，服抗焦虑的药物，让病情尽可能掌握在自己的手中。

每天坚持散步或锻炼，保持乐观的心态和行动。

注意休息和保证睡眠时间和质量。

培养令人开心快乐的兴趣和爱好。

今天就写到这里，能这样写出自己的心里话，是快乐和幸福的。

（我已经忘记了时间的记录，没有了日子的概念，不知今夕何夕）

刚刚出去海边散步回来，把汗擦干，洗个澡，人也感觉轻松愉快。

中午时不知何因就情绪低落，焦虑着，很多不健康的想法在脑子里盘旋不去，我想忍住，但不成功，我最后只好吃了半粒抗焦虑的劳拉西泮，然后上床躺下休息，迷迷糊糊中不健康的想法也渐渐消失了。

明明是向好的方面发展，思想为何仍然有那么多的悲观情绪，这些情绪不请自来，也是抑郁症患者很常见的症状，这时我更需要坚定自己的信念，让乐观思想把悲观的情绪赶走。

仿佛一场长久的战争，我和病魔每天都在对抗，有时它控制了我的情绪和思想，我就要用药物和精神力量将它赶走，当然，说时容易做时难，但只要我有一天的日子，就要和它对抗到底。

我是个不怕死的人，只是不想死得太痛苦，但谁能知道自己会怎样结束自己的生命呢？

一个人若到了不能自理的地步，是多么悲哀，明知道这样再活下去对人对己都是一种折磨，但除了了结这难以承受的痛苦，我还有什么办法好好地活下去？

我活得很痛苦，也给尼尔带来很大的困扰和压力，看到他为了照顾我而消瘦，我感到很难过，所以我也尽量不要把不健康的情绪说给他听。

我知道家人和许多朋友都在为我鼓劲和祈祷，这对我是一种安慰，也增添了我的力量和勇气。但这个病却像一个漫漫无边的黑夜，紧紧把我笼罩，令我不能动弹。

当我静下来的时候，我就会不知所措，或者胡思乱想，把很小的事情放大成没顶的灾难，身体上的小痛苦也会被放大成大问题，这是令我十分困惑的地方，所以我也常常提醒自己，问题没有我想象的那么严重，让自己放下心头的大石。

我想过了结自己生命的方法，但是还没有去实行，因为我心中还有尼尔，我舍不得离开，也不知道我若先走了，会给尼尔带来怎样的痛苦与悲伤，我不能丢下尼尔一个人孤孤单单。

病中，我失去了许多自信心，这完全不是健康的我的形象，健康的时候，无论遇见怎样的困难和波折，我都能坦然面对，但这抑郁症控制了我的思想，令我的自信心也变成了瘫痪。

那么，我还能怎样地活下去呢？

我要找些事情做，这样我就没有时间胡思乱想，写作是我喜欢的事情，那么把自己的心路历程真实记录下来，或者对来者有参考的作用。

常常是脑子一片空白，或者心里一团乱麻，理不清一个头绪，多想了还会头疼得难受，不想时间又不好打发。书和电视都看不进去，只有上网浏览新闻和体育赛事，我喜欢看女排、网球、乒乓球和羽毛球，这些赛事伴随我度过很多闲暇的时光。

论坛和微信公众号，我已经很少去参与编辑和管理了，文字的交流和心灵的共鸣，这都是我过去很喜欢玩的内容，也花费过我很多的时间和心血，现在我只能望病兴叹，去了论坛，只是默默选几个老朋友的帖子看看，一点编辑和回复交流的欲望都没有。而微信，也退到了只在朋友圈发点照片的地步，让关心我的朋友亲人们知道我仍然活着。

尼尔成了我的头脑和身体行动的操作者。

今天是2019年12月23日星期一，明天就是圣诞平安夜，也是我看医生的日子，看看Janet对我的病况有何安排。

尼尔说明年想找点义工做，以回报社会，结交一些朋友。我没有说什么，但我不知道我是否能够独自在家安好。

今晚，我们在家吃火腿和土豆色拉，很简单，吃完我们还分吃了一只芒果，芒果的味道好极了。

最近感觉视力比以前差了很多，右眼看东西很模糊，左眼还可以，可能都带有老花了，岁月不饶人，谁也脱不了生老病死的人生历程。

今年圣诞，朋友米尔兰邀请我们去午餐，我们乐意参加，拜访老朋友，认识新朋友，毕竟都是很好的，只是我不知道身体和精神到时能不能享受和朋友一起的美丽时光。

嘴巴右边上排最后一个大牙，对有酸性的水果很敏感，不知是不是有感染，我已经定了27号去给牙医检查一下，防患于未然。

尼尔问我明天看Janet怎么说？我说只是好了一点点，进展不明显，可喜的是：我已经能够写我想写的日记。所以就是这点已经令我感到脑子有用和高兴。

圣诞前夕，去看Janet，没有什么新进展，她叫我继续服药和锻炼，当有不良的想法在脑中出现，可以进行剧烈运动，然后停下来，也可拥抱自己喜欢的东西，或者用冰块放在额头上降温。也可以想三件开心的事去代替不良的想法。

圣诞节去米尔兰的家吃午饭，她的家在三一海滩边的山腰上，依山而建，风景很优美，午饭有火鸡和火腿，色拉，甜品等等，除了我和尼尔，还有三位客人：一位法官，她先生Brian和儿子Alex。

27号下午去看牙医，他给我检查了一下牙齿，牙齿没有发炎，澳洲的牙医费用真的很厉害。

最近还感觉肩部有痛感，穿衣服脱衣服都感到不舒服，可能是肩周炎，这些问题一个个出现，令人更加沮丧，这日子不知道如何过下去，这人生为什么就有这么多的苦难和波折呢？一波未平一波又起。

不管怎样，还是先把抑郁症治好为要，这病好了，其他的病就容易对付，这病不好，一切都是负担。

早上吃过早餐，本想做午餐的饭盒，但由于鸡肉没有解冻好，所以推迟到下午或者明天进行。

这几天晚上睡眠还可以，所以白天的精神也好些，也能写下一些这样的日记。

回看自己打字的内容，思维还是比较清晰，比较有条理的，不是混乱到像一个疯子一样，所以这也是我感到高兴的事情，如果思维混乱，那就真的是疯子了，那样会更加悲哀。

写下这一页多的文字，脑子就感到疲劳了，一点也不像以前健康时的写作状态，这样写着写着就想睡觉，要提起精神就这么难吗？

幸亏我还能动脑子打字，否则和一个植物人没有两样，如果成了植物人，人生的乐趣就完全失去了，这样活着，害人害己，不如早点归于尘土，但结束一个生命，也不是那么容易的事情，半死不活的，真是难受。

尼尔刚进我房间，说他感到不舒服，可能是感冒了，他服了药，看看能不能解决问题。

下午心血来潮，去家附近的游泳馆加入会员，每周约16澳币的费用，一年花费800多元，就作为锻炼和恢复健康的投资吧。

办好手续后立马跳进泳池游泳,很久没有游了,所以游得很费劲,但因为是自己想做的事情,所以很开心,以后希望每天都能保持进泳池游泳,但愿天公不负有心人,给我一条生路,让我健健康康活下去,否则真的很难坚持面对抑郁症了。

游泳回到家里,上楼腿很沉,第一天泳,肯定是要适应的,相信游多几天会舒服起来。

头脑还是有点昏昏沉沉,说明恢复得还不够利索,想看论坛的帖子也不是很流畅,不知还有什么办法能够快点好起来。

今天是2019年12月29日星期天,早上起床吃过早餐,就给自己做午餐饭盒,做好已经是中午十二点,我穿好泳裤就去游泳池游泳。在温暖的泳池游是最舒服的,我只会泳蛙泳,泳池里有几个人在泡泳,享受周日的闲暇,我也很悠闲地游了半个小时,这时天空下起了密密的雨,有一片天还是蓝色的,所以应该是过云雨,果然我去换完衣服出来,雨再下一会儿就停了,太阳也转出了云层,我就拿去背囊走回家。

尼尔过来问我觉得如何,我说挺不错。然后我边吃个饭盒当午餐,吃完再吃一条香蕉,然后便是午睡时间。因为今天的运动量已经完成,所以我放心睡了一个长觉,一直到五点钟才起床。

我听到尼尔咳嗽和擤鼻涕,估计感冒还没好,我过去探其感觉如何:主要是咳嗽和流涕比较烦人。

我今天早上就感觉不好,很多不好的念头不受控制地在脑海里盘旋,令人厌倦人生,忧郁这老狐狸又跳出来控制和考验我,令我感觉真的很悲观,看不见康复的希望在哪里?每天的服药只是吊着半条命而已。但悲观又能如何?要寻短见吧,我是绝对不能抛下尼尔孤单一个人面对世界,这样想来,只能尽量以积极的态度来面对每天的生活。

医生说我服用的度洛斯叮每天180ml已经是她能开出的最大剂量，不会再加大了，没有病人达到过这个剂量，但我的病还是不见大好，除了这种药，不知道还有没有其他的药可以尝试呢？想到这里，我又不禁有点担忧未来，人生活到这个地步，真的很难，活也不成，不活也不成。

总是感觉自己下半生的结局悲惨，一切苦难因为得了抑郁症，我这样没有自理的能力，他日尼尔的身体若有三长两短，我病情还不变好，我就只有坐而待毙了，真的不敢往下想下去，我为何会得这种病？这比癌症更加折磨人，癌症会有尽期，我不怕死，但就怕这种不死不活的状况，万能的主啊，我一生为人忠厚善良，从来没有做过亏心事，为什么老头爷拿这个顽疾来折磨我？我诚意请求你放我一条活路好吗？

看来，我只能以不变应万变，趁现在脑子还算清醒，写下自己的真切感受，让后人多了解病人的真实情况，共同找到比较有效的应对方法。

我一直热爱人生，但如果病成现在这个样子，我宁愿早点归化尘土。

写下这短短的文字，脑袋就感觉很沉重，没有了往日的轻灵和诗意的美丽，一个热爱写字的人，没有了写作的健康头脑，是多么悲哀的事情；一个摄影师，没有了健康的身体，走遍万水千山，用镜头去记录人生和生活的喜怒哀乐，是多么悲哀的事情，这些令人感觉生活美好的开心事，都因为抑郁症的控制，而成了不可实现的梦想，我还能干些什么来度过这漫长的日子？总不成每天二十四小时都在迷迷糊糊的睡眠中度过？

我刚写下一些杂感，但马上就忘记写了些什么，这病把我的记忆力大大删除了，许多英文字都记不起来，就算会读也拼不起来，这样我的自信心不由得就受到了打击，写几个字填个表都填不来，我还能干些什么，自理些什么？

思想就是这样迷迷糊糊地，日子也是这样迷迷糊糊地过，我感觉自己这次最终逃不过抑郁症对我的毁灭，也不知道还有多长的折磨和多艰难的困苦在等着我。

再过两天，就是新的一年了，2020年，希望有奇迹发生在我的身上，请求万能的主给我勇气和力量。毕竟，我确实是个非常热爱生命的人。

今天早上十一点就去游泳锻炼，回到家里是中午十二点，不知道为什么心里总有不好的思想在浮现，赶也赶不走，很讨厌这种状态，很多次对自己说不能有自毁的念头，但被抑郁这个魔鬼控制的时候却怎么也躲不开这种情绪。这抑郁症就有这种强迫病人胡思乱想的力量，叫人防不胜防，非常的无能为力。

记得医生叮嘱我有不好想法时要剧烈运动，或者额头加冰，拥抱喜欢的东西，想几件令自己开心的事情，道理都很明白，但试了收效不大，我用了跳绳，拥抱小熊，写东西和看视频等转移注意力。

现在因为听力受到很大的破坏，所以看电视听不懂对白的内容，也定不下心神观看节目，日子每一天都不好过。但也想不出更好的办法来应对。

2019 的最后一天，我早起时尼尔已经去超市，我吃过早餐，清理了洗碗机里面的杯盘碗碟，不久尼尔提着许多购物袋回家了。帮助清理完袋子里的东西，快十二点了，我便换好泳裤去游泳馆锻炼去了。

今天泳池里游泳的人较周末的少，所以我可以舒舒服服地游蛙泳，每次游五十米就歇一歇，然后再游五十米，这样来来回回游到十二点四十分，我便出水，拿起背囊换衣服去了，擦干身子上的水，更衣完毕，我便走回家来。

今天不像昨天脑子里有那么多不良的思想，吃了饭我便回房午睡去了，一觉醒来，已经是下午五点钟，我也不急，总之闲着也是闲着，像个残疾人一样活着，我还能对自己有什么更好的要求呢，承认这病一时还医治不好，能够活着就已经是一种奇迹了，头脑还是这样一时清醒一时糊涂，想多了头痛，不想又像个白痴，Janet啊，你一定要救救我，我把所有的希望都寄托在你的身上了。

每天都坚持写几行字，就当是保持大脑的活动，也填补大把大把的空余时间，否则得空了，仍然会胡思乱想的，什么时候身体感觉舒服的时候，想法一般都是积极乐观的，当看不见希望和身体感觉不适的时候，情绪就是不良和悲观的。

一年多的坚持，走到今天是多么的不容易，回想，真不知道自己是怎么熬过来的，要有多坚强，才能坚持到这一刻。而未来，还能不能好起来，心中一点谱都没有，每个医生都说我会好起来的，但现在一年多过去了，我仍然是这样不死不活的样子，我内心的焦虑是可以理解的，也怪不得自己如此的绝望，但我很高兴我还没有放弃我的生命，我心中还有对尼尔的爱与希望。

六号那天，又去看医生Janet，告诉她我现在病情不上不下的状况，希望她给我一点新希望。她说再加一款抗抑郁的并且可以帮助睡眠的药给我服用，如果还不见效果，她建议我去医院进行ECT电疗，她说这个疗效很好，如果她家人朋友像我现在这样，她也会建议他们接受这种治疗。

这种方法听起来非常吓人：用真电电击脑子，天啊！但退后再想，如果全身麻醉，也没有什么可怕的，醉了啥事都不知道了，醒来就是另一番境界，对吧，最坏的打算就是离开这个世界，这样也挺好的，免得活得这么难受。

昨晚服了医生开的新药，睡了一个很美好的觉，今天觉得精神挺好的，头脑也比较清醒，和尼尔去超市购物，脑子也没有什么问题，中午回到家里，便拿起背囊去游泳。泳池不太拥挤，我游了一会蛙泳，便练习一会自由泳，时间很快便过了一点钟，我擦干身子，回到家已经是一点半了，我感觉饿了，便打开冰箱拿出一块香蕉蛋糕当午餐吃，之前一直吃鸡肉白饭当午餐，换一下口味也是非常不错的，不喜欢可以再换回来。

吃完蛋糕我就上床睡觉，一直睡到下午五点多，没睡着，就是不想睁开眼睛，忽然记起一个红袖天涯论坛一起玩过的朋友，她的名字叫手指一勾，后来又有一个马甲叫作灵魂进化，我还是感觉勾勾的名字更加亲切，能记起一个老朋友的名字，使我感觉自己的病情好像又有了转机，我想，如果我也能记起其他许多人事，是不是就是离康复不远了呢？想到这里，心情竟然就舒畅起来，仿佛看到了希望的那道光。

然后我便上论坛去看看，好像这几天风起云涌，战火纷飞，然后有些朋友倒下，或者离开，或者告别，然后还开始倒版，哈哈，这班人真是吃饱了撑的，不点火生事好像就活不下去了。我也乐得看热闹，我很惊讶我能集中精神读一些帖子，也能记得一些读过的内容，所以感觉还是挺快乐的。活生生的人，活生生的事，活生生的喜怒哀乐。

也许昨晚开始服的药，就是给我带来转机的良方，记得医生也说过，我的病有的医治，只要找到对的药，所以我等的就是这样的良药。希望我服了这药，一天天好起来，那样的话，就是一个大大的奇迹。

能写的时候，我就写这个手记，记录自己经历着的事情，什么时候病好了，还是快离开了，也忠实记录下来。病了一年零四个月，不知自己是怎么挺过来的，很难熬的岁月，如果可以挑选我真的不想这样废人一般活着。

但既然一时还死不掉，那就赖活，能过多久便多久。尼尔在我身边是我最感幸福的事情，他每天这样不离不弃照顾我，让我万分感动，他对我的大恩大德，我这辈子也回报不了。

如果没有尼尔对我的悉心照料，我不会活到今天，抑郁症是如此难对付的一种病，普通人根本难以明白病人的感受，更别说感同身受了，许多令人费解的反常思想和行为，作为家人也是一种折磨，相信许多人都经不起这么困难的身心考验，但尼尔确实尽到了一个伴侣最感动人的责任，这是我想都不敢想的境况。

我的病每一种改善和进步都与尼尔的关爱和努力紧紧联系在一起。我最亲爱的尼尔噢，感激一生遇见你，我俩在一起的经历，是人间最美的一段爱情，没有你，就早已经没有我，所以现在每一天我都在感恩中度过。

2020年1月19日，星期天。

早上起床就觉得心情不太好，满脑子不良的思想，挺糟糕的，所以我吃完早餐，做了几个午餐饭盒后，便去游泳，希望运动赶走不良的想法。不知何故，我脑子里就是充满了不想这样活下去的念头，而且非常难于摆脱它的影响，抑郁这只恶魔啊，随时随地都会跳出来折磨我考验我的耐力与毅力。

游泳时游了一百米蛙泳，再游五十米自由泳，歇歇，然后再游五十米自由泳，接着就放慢速度在水里或走或游，这样半小时的运动很快就过去了，到更衣室换了衣服，此时恰好是正午，太阳很猛，气温35度，我打起雨伞遮阳，慢慢走回家来。

游泳后，有点累，但身心都很舒畅，那些不良的思想也不知不觉溜走了，我用毛巾擦干身体上的汗水，然后吃一块香蕉蛋糕作午餐，吃完再吃一枚黑色的李子作结。

午餐后人感到特别困，我告诉尼尔我去休息了，便上床睡觉，迷迷糊糊睡了一个下午，直到傍晚六点多才醒，今晚尼尔准备做比萨，我不喜欢吃，所以我准备吃中午自己做好的海鲜与白饭。

我吃了一条香蕉，和尼尔在客厅里聊了一会儿，就到七点了，于是我将准备好的饭菜放入微波炉热了两分钟，然后就在餐桌上用晚餐，晚餐后吃了一个苹果，再加几颗洋李脯，这对服药造成的便秘有一定效果。

这几天我一直觉得自己写不出太多的字句，所以没有动笔，刚才忽然想起医生的叮嘱，要我逼一下自己多想和多写，所以我便再次打开这个话题，接着写下去，写了什么，脑子一点也记不清楚，但我可以写下这些，说明我的头脑还是清醒的，思维也没有混乱，心理上的不自信都是由于抑郁症的折磨而起的。

不管怎样，我能写下这些字，我感到还有一些希望，至少我还没有变成疯子。当然，写这些字要花比较多精神，不像平时写作时的轻松自如。

精神不够集中，心神散乱，记忆模糊，这是我现在常常遇见的问题，读一段文字，读过了马上就忘记，英文的内容也是模模糊糊地在脑海里掠过，许多英文单词都记不起来，所以阅读与理解也就成了困难，我也很沮丧自己脑子运用起来的这种状态，但沮丧了又能如何？

Janet医生因为要开会,所以要到本月底才能给我看病,我本月中去看了我的GP,Natasha Crees,她给我量了血压和做了心电图,结果都很正常。她给我加了点药量,叮嘱我若有不良的事情发生我可以再来看她,我点了点头。

以我这样的状况,我到底应不应该去做ECT电疗呢?我也不太懂,医生说如果她有亲友像我这种情况,她一定建议他们去电疗。我有点担心,但也想尝试一下这种方法,否则像现在这样半死不活地活着,真的很难受,至少有尝试才会有希望,即使失败了,也毕竟曾经尝试过。

现在我的情况是做不好文字和图文编辑工作的,心有余而力不足,也管理不了论坛,至于摄影我的最爱,也放停了脚步,很久没有拿起相机出去拍照了,感觉辜负了凯恩斯大好的风光。

就说家门口那棵高大茂密的玉桂树,花也开得正好,就是没有精神和力气拿起相机出门给花们留下美丽动人的美态。

不敢去想将来,因为以我目前的状况,到哪里都会成为一种负累,而这又恰恰是自己和别人都负担不起的。那么我又能何去何从呢?要是死有那么容易,我倒是不留恋生命,只要我不给别人和社会留下太多的麻烦和负担,我愿意承担自己的责任。说到这里,我不由得再次皱起眉头,要摆脱困境,必须在治疗上有所突破,否则只有看着自己一天天沉沦下去。

我想我还是应该同意医生的提议,去试一次听起来非常吓人但据说效果非常不错的电疗吧,于是我把我的想法和尼尔商量,尼尔也觉得应该试一试,至少还有这个最后的希望。

万能的上帝或万能的老天爷啊,求您给我指点迷津,给我一条充满生机的生路,让我在濒临绝境中起死回生,您老人家知道,我还有很多美景没有拍照,很多靓仔靓女没有欣赏够,很多美食还没有来得及做来吃咧!如果我能够凤凰涅槃,我一定不会令您失望,一定会为人类和社会做出更多更大的贡献的,信不信由您!

Foreword

My name is Bizi. Unfortunately, I suffer from severe depression. Everything in my body and life has changed beyond recognition.

The mind is groggy all day long, like sleeping, and the anxiety and uneasiness generated all the time is painful.

It has become a habit to take medicine. A lot of medicine is swallowed in order to have a peaceful day.

Duluostin is the main antidepressant. I now take 150mg every day, plus and Lamiton. This is my daily homework. medicine is not less.

The days of illness are very difficult every day.

I can't decide to read and watch TV, and writing is today: Sunday, December 22, 2019, I just started to try again, hoping to regain my old joy and fill my spare time. It also drives away the crankiness and weakness that comes to mind from time to time.

The doctor said that I will get better slowly. I need patience and persistence, and at the same time keep exercising. Whenever I feel

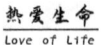
Love of Life

good, I believe her, but when I feel uncomfortable, my brain and body are not working, I become more pessimistic.

I now sleep or try to sleep most of the time every day, because only sleep makes me feel that time is easier to spend, 1 sleep relieve my worries. When I don't find other good ways, I will still sleep every day. Spend.

Writing these words today makes me feel that my thinking is still organized and clear, which gives me great confidence and encouragement. In this way, I can easily fill my leisure time.

I believe that if I can write one page, I can write ten pages and more words.

The feeling of being controlled by depression is extremely painful. People who have not experienced this kind of torture can hardly imagine their symptoms. Many people still think that this is just a little melancholy in their hearts. As long as they relax their mood, everything will be relieved and their illness will be better. If depression is as people think, then not so many patients have to choose to kill themselves to end their lives and pain. I feel the same way now. I understand very well that these people's choices are forced and understandable.

Since September last year, I have been tortured to death by depression. I have lived like a walking corpse for a long time. I have also thought about suicide many times and been freed. However, Neil would be lonely in Keynes without me. I can't bear to leave alone and live as long as I can.

Now I go for a walk by the sea with Neil every evening. Every time I go home after a walk, I sweat slightly and feel relaxed and happy. People really need to exercise or walk around to activate their muscles and bones, breathe fresh air and strengthen blood circulation. After all, it is good for their health.

In retrospect, my depression was caused by long-term insomnia. The taste of long-term insomnia was really uncomfortable. I have not found a good drug to improve my sleep so far. But there is a herbal capsule called Sleep EZY, which has helped me sleep at night without any bad side effects.

I haven't updated our WeChat public number platform for a long time. Because of the repeated depression, I had to give up the development of the platform temporarily. I was in poor spirits. Without the maintenance of the platform, I naturally lost a lot of communication and fun in life.

I can write the above words today to prove that my physical condition has improved. I want to enjoy the hard-won moment and strive to record my own experiences and thoughts, as to let readers have a deeper understanding of depression and a better understanding of the pain and difficulty of patients.

For the patient, the understanding of the family is very important, because many of the patient's experiences and conditions seem incredible, for example: patients often lose confidence in life because they can't see any hope of survival. Patients will be controlled by the disease and deprived of the ability to survive, so that their mind and body paralysis, can not think and act, lose the power of life. In addition, depression will also undermine the confidence and courage of patients in many ways, prompting patients to end their lives.

The patient's physical examination is normal for many times,

热爱生命
Love of Life

but the problem appears in the spirit, and the illness is also distracted by and physical function. There are many examples of psychogenic illness, such as emotional loss of control, environmental changes, unexpected events, etc. My illness belongs to the weakness of neurological function, causing insomnia, and then depression caused by long-term insomnia.

There are also many side effects of antidepressants. Constipation is one of them. Therefore, we always have drugs and food for defecation at home and pay attention to drinking more water at ordinary times. There is also the drug can cause low blood pressure, stand up often feel dizzy, after a while to return to normal.

Patients have to fight with the disease every day. They cannot be completely controlled by the disease in their thoughts and actions. When they have the opportunity, they must let themselves master and control in turn, give themselves confidence and courage, and believe that doctors and drugs will help them restore their health and bring themselves happiness.

Take antidepressants on time and in the amount every day. When you encounter anxiety, take anti-anxiety drugs to keep the condition in your own hands as much as possible.

Take a walk or exercise every day and keep an optimistic attitude and action.

Pay attention to rest and ensure sleep time and quality.

Cultivate happy interests and hobbies.

Today, I will write here. It is happy and happy to be able to write my own heart in this way.

(I have forgotten the record of time, without the concept of day, I don't know what evening is this evening)

I just came back from a walk on the beach, dried my sweat and took a bath. I also felt relaxed and happy.

At noon, I felt depressed and anxious for some reason. Many unhealthy thoughts hovered in my mind. I wanted to hold back, but I didn't succeed. I finally had to take half a anti-anxiety lorazepam, then go to bed and lie down to rest. The unhealthy thoughts in my daze gradually disappeared.

Obviously, it is developing for the better. Why are there still so many pessimism in my mind? These uninvited emotions are also very common symptoms of depression patients. At this time, I need to strengthen my beliefs and let optimistic thoughts drive away pessimism.

It seems that 1 is a long-term war. I am fighting with the disease every day. Sometimes it controls my emotions and thoughts. I will use drugs and spiritual strength to drive it away. Of course, it is easier said than done, but as long as I have One day, we must fight it to the end.

I am a person who is not afraid of death, just don't want to die too painful, but who can know how to end their own life?

How sad it is for a person to be unable to take care of himself. Knowing that living like this is 1 torture to others and oneself, but apart from ending this unbearable pain, how can I live well?

I lived a miserable life and brought Neil a lot of trouble and pressure. I felt very sad to see him lose weight in order to take care of me, so I also tried not to tell him about unhealthy emotions.

I know that my family and many friends are encouraging and praying for me. This is 1 a kind of comfort to me, and it also

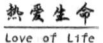

adds strength and courage to me. But this disease is like a long and boundless night, tightly shrouded me, so that I can not move.

When I calm down, I will be at a loss, or cranky, magnifying small things into unsolved disasters, and small physical pains will also be magnified into big problems. This is a place that makes me very confused. Therefore, I often remind myself that the problem is not as serious as I thought, so let myself put down the big stone in my heart.

I thought about the way to end my life, but I haven't implemented it yet, because I still have Neil in my heart. I can't bear to leave, and I don't know what kind of pain and sadness I will bring to Neil if I leave first. I can't leave Neil alone.

During the illness, I lost a lot of self-confidence. This is not a healthy image of me at all. When I am healthy, no matter what difficulties and twists and turns I encounter, I can face them calmly, but this depression has controlled my thoughts and made me My self-confidence has also become paralyzed.

How can I live?

I want to find something to do, so that I don't have time to think about it. Writing is my favorite thing, so I can really record my mental journey or have a reference effect on the comers.

Often my mind is blank, or my heart is in a mess, and I can't figure out a clue. If I think about it, I will have a headache. I don't want to spend time. I can't watch books or TV. I can only browse news and sports events on the Internet. I like watching women's volleyball, tennis, table tennis and badminton. These events accompany me to spend a lot of leisure time.

I have rarely participated in editing and management of

forums and WeChat public numbers. The exchange of words and the resonance of my heart are all content that I used to like to play, and I have spent a lot of time and effort. Now I can only look at my illness and sigh. I went to the forum. I just silently selected the posts of a few old friends to and read. I have no desire to edit and reply to communicate. WeChat, on the other hand, has also retreated to the point of only sending some photos in the circle of friends to let my friends and relatives who care about me know that I am still alive.

Neil became the operator of my mind and body actions.

Today is Monday, December 23, 2019. Tomorrow is Christmas Eve. It is also the day when I see a doctor to see what Janet has to do with my condition.

Neil explained that he wanted to find some volunteers to do in order to give back to the society and make some friends. I didn't say anything, but I don't know if I can be safe at home alone.

Tonight, we ate ham and potato salad at home. It was very simple. After eating, we also ate 1 mangoes. Mangoes tasted very good.

Recently, I feel that my eyesight is much worse than before. I can see things in my right eye and my left eye is fine. I may have presbyopia. No one can escape the life course of birth, old age, sickness and death.

This Christmas, my friend Milland invited us to lunch. We are willing to attend, visit old friends and meet new friends. After all, it is all very good, but I don't know if I can enjoy the beautiful time with my friends physically and mentally.

The last big tooth on the right side of the mouth is very sensitive to acidic fruits. I don't know if there is any infection. I have already

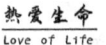
Love of Life

ordered the 27th to have it checked by the dentist to take precautions.

Neil asked me I 'd watch tomorrow. What 'd Janet say? I said it was only a little better, the progress was not obvious, and the good news was that I had been able to write the diary I wanted to write. So this is what has made me feel useful and happy.

On Christmas Eve, I went to see Janet. There was no new progress. She told me to continue taking medicine and exercising. When bad thoughts appeared in my mind, I could do strenuous exercise, then stop, hug something I liked, or put ice cubes on my forehead to cool down. You can also think of three happy things to replace bad thoughts.

Christmas went to Millan's home for lunch. Her home is on the mountainside beside Trinity Beach. It is built on the mountain. The scenery is very beautiful. There are turkey and ham, salad, dessert and so on for lunch. Besides Neil and I, there are also three guests: the 1 judge, her husband Brian and his son Alex.

On the afternoon of the 27th, I went to see a dentist. He checked my teeth. The teeth were not inflamed. The cost of dentists in Australia is really high.

Recently, I also feel pain in my shoulder. I feel uncomfortable when I wear clothes and take off clothes. It may be frozen shoulder. These problems appear one by one, which makes people more depressed. I don't know how to live these days. Why is there so much suffering and twists and turns in this life? One wave after another.

In any case, it is necessary to cure depression first. If this disease is cured, other diseases will be easy to deal with. If this disease is not good, everything is a burden.

After breakfast in the morning, I wanted to make a lunch box, but because the chicken was not defrosted well, it was postponed until the afternoon or tomorrow.

I can sleep well these days, so I feel better during the day and can write down some diaries like this.

Looking back at the content of my typing, my thinking is still clearer and more organized. It is not chaotic to like a madman. Therefore, this is also something I am happy about. If my thinking is chaotic, it is really madman's, which will be even sadder.

After writing these 1 pages of words, my brain will feel tired. It is not at all like the writing state when I was healthy before. If I write like this, I want to sleep. Is it so difficult to lift my spirits?

Fortunately, I can still use my brain to type, otherwise I am no different from a vegetable. If I become a vegetable, the joy of life will be completely lost. If I live like this and harm others and myself, it is better to return to the dust earlier, but it is not so easy to end a life. It is really uncomfortable to be half dead.

Neil had just come into my room and said he wasn't feeling well, maybe he had a cold, and he took medicine to see if it would solve the problem.

On a whim in the afternoon, I went to the swimming pool near my home to join the membership. The cost is about 16 Australian dollars a week, and it costs more than 800 yuan a year as an investment in exercise and recovery.

After completing the formalities, I immediately jumped into the swimming pool to swim. I haven't swum for a long time, so I swam very hard, but because it is what I want to do, I am very happy. I hope

热爱生命
Love of Life

I can keep swimming in the swimming pool every day in the future. I hope God will live up to my heart and give me a way to live healthily, otherwise it is really difficult to persist in facing depression.

When I came home from swimming, my legs were very heavy when I went upstairs. I must get used to swimming on the first day. I believe I will feel comfortable after swimming for a few more days.

The mind is still a little groggy, indicating that the recovery is not quick enough, and the of the posts that want to see the forum is not very smooth. I don't know what else can be done to get better quickly.

Today is Sunday, December 29, 2019. I got up in the morning and had breakfast. I made lunch boxes for myself. It was already 12 noon. I put on my swimming trunks and went swimming in the swimming pool. Swimming in the warm swimming pool is the most comfortable. I can only swim breaststroke. There are a few people in the swimming pool swimming to and enjoy the leisure time on Sunday. I also swam leisurely for half an hour. At this moment, the sky began to rain densely. The sky was still blue for a while, so it should be cloudy and rainy. Sure enough, I went to change my clothes and stopped the rain, the sun also turned out of the clouds, so I took it to my backpack and walked home.

Neil came and asked me how I felt, and I said it was good. Then I eat a lunch box for lunch, eat a banana after eating, and then it is nap time. Because today's exercise has been completed, so I rest assured that a long sleep, until five o'clock to get up.

I heard Neil cough and blow his nose. I think his cold is still not over. I went to find out how he felt: mainly coughing and runny nose are annoying.

一个抑郁症患者的手记
Notes of a depressed patient

I felt bad this morning. Many bad thoughts hovered in my mind uncontrollably, which made me tired of life. The old fox of melancholy jumped out to control and test me again, making me feel really pessimistic and unable to see where the hope of recovery is? The daily medication is just hanging half a life. But what about pessimism? To be short-sighted, I absolutely can't leave Neil alone to face the world. In this way, I can only try my best to face daily life with a positive attitude.

The doctor said that the –degree of Los Ding I took was already of the maximum doses she could prescribe, and it would not be increased any more. No patient had reached this dose, but my illness was still not very good. Apart from this medicine, I wonder if there are any other drugs to try? When I think of this, I can't help but worry about the future. It's really hard to live to this point in life. I can't live, and I can't live without it.

I always feel that the end of the rest of my life is miserable. All the sufferings are due to depression. I have no ability to take care of myself. If anything happens to Neil's body and my condition is not good, I will have to sit and wait for death. I really dare not think about it. Why do I get this disease? This is more painful than cancer. Cancer will have period. I am not afraid of death, but I am afraid of this situation of immortality. Almighty Lord, I have been honest and kind all my life and have never done anything wrong. Why does the old man torment me with this stubborn disease? I'm asking you to let me live, okay?

It seems that I can only respond to changes with the same, while my mind is still clear, write down my true feelings, so that future generations can know more about the real situation of the patient and find a more effective way to deal with it.

I have always loved life, but if illness to what it is now, I would rather naturalize the dust earlier.

Write this short text, the head feels very heavy, without the light spirit and poetic beauty of the past, a person who loves to write, without a healthy mind for writing, how sad it is; a photographer, without a healthy body, travels all over the rivers and mountains, using the lens to record the joys and sorrows of life and life, how sad things, these happy things that make people feel that life is beautiful, because of the control of depression, it has become an unrealized dream. What else can I do to spend this long day? Can't you spend 24 hours a day in a daze?

I just wrote down some miscellaneous feelings, but I immediately forgot what I wrote. This disease has greatly deleted my memory. I can't remember many English words, even if I can read them, I can't spell them. In this way, my self-confidence can't help but be hit. I can't fill in a form with a few words. What else can I do and what can I do take care of myself?

The thought is in such a daze, and the life is also in such a daze. I feel that I can't escape the destruction of depression this time, and I don't know how long the torture and hardship are waiting for me.

In two days, it will be a new year. In 2020, I hope a miracle will happen to me and ask the Almighty to give me courage and strength. After all, I am really a person who loves life.

I went swimming at eleven o'clock this morning. It was twelve o'clock at noon when I got home. I don't know why there are always bad thoughts in my heart. I can't catch them. I hate this state very much. I told myself many times that I can't have the idea of self-destruction, but when I was controlled by the devil of depression, I couldn't avoid this emotion. This depression has the power to force the patient to think, which is overwhelming and very powerless.

I remember the doctor told me to take strenuous exercise when I had bad ideas, or add ice to my forehead, hug what I liked, and a few things that made me happy. The reason was very clear, but the results were not good. I used rope skipping, hugging bears, writing and watching videos to divert my attention.

Now because of the great damage to hearing, so watching TV can not understand the content of the dialogue, also can not settle down to watch the program, every day is difficult. But I can't think of a better way to deal with it.

On the last day of 2019, when I got up early, Neil had already gone to the supermarket. I had breakfast and cleaned the cups and dishes in the dishwasher. Soon Neil came home with many shopping bags. Help clean up the contents of the bag, it was almost twelve o'clock, I changed my swimming trunks and went to the swimming pool for exercise.

There are fewer swimmers in the swimming pool today than on weekends, so I can swim breaststroke comfortably. I take a rest every time I swim 50 meters, and then swim another 50 meters. in this way, I swim back and forth until 12: 40, then I get out of the water, pick up my backpack and change clothes, dry the water on my body, and walk home after changing clothes.

Today, I don't have so many bad thoughts in my mind as

热爱生命
Love of Life

yesterday. After eating, I went back to my room to take a nap. 1 I woke up, it was already five o'clock in the afternoon, and I was not in a hurry. In short, I was also idle, living like a disabled person. What better can I ask of myself? Admitting that this disease is not cured for a while, it is already a 1 miracle to be alive, the mind is still so clear and confused for a while, thinking too much headache, don't want to be like an idiot again, Janet, you must help me, I put all my hopes on you.

If you insist on writing a few lines every day, you should keep your brain active and fill a lot of spare time. Otherwise, if you are empty, you will still think wildly. When your body feels comfortable, your thoughts are generally positive and optimistic. When you can't see hope and feel uncomfortable, your mood is bad and pessimistic.

After more than a year of persistence, it is not easy to get to today. Looking back, I really don't know how I got through it and how strong I have to be to stick to this moment. In the future, I have no idea whether I can get better or not. Every doctor said that I will get better. But now more than a year later, I am still so immortal. My inner anxiety is understandable. No wonder I am so desperate. But I am glad that I have not given up my life. I still have love and hope for Neil.

On the 6th, I went to see the doctor again, Janet, and told her that I was in a serious condition. I hope she can give me some new hope. She said that she would add 1 antidepressant and sleep-helping drugs to me. If it didn't work, she suggested that I go to the hospital for ECT electrotherapy. She said that the effect was very good. If her family and friends were like me now, she would also suggest that they accept this treatment.

This method sounds very scary: shock the brain with real electricity, for God's sake! But back and think again, if the general anesthesia, there is nothing to be afraid of, drunk what all don't know, wake up is another state, right, the worst plan is to leave the world, this is also very good, so as not to live so uncomfortable.

Last night, I took the new medicine prescribed by the doctor and had a good sleep., today I feel very energetic and clear-headed. I went shopping with Neil in the supermarket and had no brain problems. When I got home at noon, I picked up my backpack and went swimming. The swimming pool was not too crowded. I swam breaststroke for a while and practiced freestyle for a while. The time soon passed one o'clock. I dried my body and it was already one thirty when I got home. I felt hungry, so I opened the refrigerator and took out a piece of banana cake for lunch. I had always eaten chicken rice for lunch before. It was also very good to change the taste. I didn't like it and could change it back.

After eating the cake, I went to bed and slept until more than five o'clock in the afternoon. I didn't fall asleep. I just didn't want to open my eyes. I suddenly remembered a friend who had played together in the Red Sleeve Tianya Forum. Her name was Finger 1 Hook. Later, there was a vest called Soul Evolution. I still felt that Hook's name was more cordial. I could remember the name of an old friend, which made me feel like another change, I think, if I can remember many other personnel, is it not far from recovery? Thought of here, the mood actually relaxed, as if to see the light of hope.

Then I went to the forum to have a look. It seemed that the wind was surging and the war was raging these days. Then some friends fell

热爱生命
Love of Life

down, or left, or said goodbye, and then began to reverse the version of. Ha ha, this group of people are really full of support. It seems that can't live without ignition and. I am also happy to watch the scene of bustle. I am surprised that I can concentrate on reading some of posts and remember some of the content I have read, so I feel quite happy. Living people, living things, living joys and sorrows.

Maybe the medicine I started to take last night is a good way to bring me a turn for the better. I remember the doctor also said that as long as I find the right medicine, I am waiting for such a good medicine. I hope I take this medicine and get better day by day. In that case, it will be a great miracle.

When I can write, I will write this note to record what I have experienced, when I am well, or when I am about to leave, and I will record it faithfully. I have been ill for one year and four months. I don't know how I survived. It's a very difficult time. If I can choose, I really don't want to live like this.

However, since we cannot die for a while, we will depend on to live as long as we can. Neil's being by my side is the happiest thing for me. He takes care of me like this every day, which makes me very touched. I can't repay his kindness to me in my life.

Without Neil's careful care for me, I would not live to this day. Depression is the 1 disease that is so difficult to deal with. It is difficult for ordinary people to understand the patient's feelings, let alone empathize. Many puzzling abnormal thoughts and behaviors, as a family member, 1 is also a kind of torture. I believe many people can't stand such a difficult physical and mental test, But Neil did fulfill the most touching responsibility of a partner, this is a situation I dare not even think about.

Every improvement and progress 1 my illness is closely linked to Neil's love and hard work. My dearest Neil Oh, I am grateful to meet you in my life. Our experience together is the most beautiful love in the world. Without you, there would have been no me, so now I spend every day in gratitude.

Sunday, January 19, 2020.

When I got up in the morning, I felt that I was not in a good mood and full of bad thoughts. It was very bad, so after I finished breakfast and made a few lunch boxes, I went swimming, hoping that exercise would drive away bad thoughts. Somehow, my mind is full of thoughts that I don't want to live like this, and it is very difficult to get rid of its influence. Depression, a demon, will come out to torture me anytime and anywhere to test my endurance and perseverance.

When swimming, I swam the 100-meter breaststroke, then the 50-meter freestyle, took a rest, then swam the 50-meter freestyle, then slowed down and walked or swam in the water. The half-hour exercise passed quickly and I changed my clothes in the dressing room. It happened to be noon. The sun was very strong and the temperature was 35 degrees. I took an umbrella to shade the sun and walked home slowly.

After swimming, I was a little tired, but my body and mind were very comfortable. Those bad thoughts slipped away unconsciously. I wiped the sweat off my body with a towel, then ate a piece of banana cake for lunch, and then ate 1 black plums for knots.

After lunch, people felt very sleepy. I told Neil that I had gone to rest and went to bed. I slept in a daze for an afternoon. I didn't wake up until more than 6 o'clock evening. Neil was going to make pizza tonight. I didn't like it, so I was going to eat seafood and rice made by myself at noon.

I ate a banana and chatted with Neil in the living room for a while. It was seven o'clock. So I put the prepared food in the microwave oven for two minutes, then I had dinner on the table. After dinner, I ate an apple and added a few preserved foreign plum, which had a certain effect on constipation caused by taking medicine.

I have been feeling that I can't write too many words these days, so I didn't write. Just now I suddenly remembered the doctor's advice, asking me to force myself to think more and write more, so I opened the topic again and went on writing. I can't remember what I wrote at all, but I can write these, which shows that my mind is still clear and my thinking is not confused, psychological lack of confidence is due to the torture of depression.

In any case, I can write these words, and I feel that there is still some hope that at least I have not become a madman. Of course, it takes more energy to write these words, unlike the ease and ease of writing at ordinary times.

The spirit is not concentrated enough, the mind is scattered, and the memory is vague. This is the problem that I often encounter now. After reading a passage, I immediately forget it. The English content is also vaguely passing in mind. Many English words are not remembered, so reading and understanding have become difficult. I am also very frustrated with this state of using my brain, but what can I do if I am frustrated?

Dr. Janet will not be able to see me until the end of this month because he has a meeting. I went to see my GP in the middle of this month and Natasha Crees. She took my blood pressure and ECG, and the results were normal. She added some medicine to me and told me that if something bad happened, I could come to see her again. I nodded.

In my situation, should I do ECT electrotherapy? I don't quite understand either. The doctor said that if she had relatives and friends like me, she would definitely suggest them to go to electrotherapy. I am a little worried, but I also want to try this method. Otherwise, it is really hard to live half-dead like this. At least there is hope only if I try. Even if I fail, I have tried it before.

At present, my situation is that I can't do a good job of editing text and pictures. I have more than enough heart and less ability to manage the forum. As for photography, my favorite, I put it and stopped. I haven't picked up my camera for a long time and went out to take pictures. I feel that I have failed to live up to Keynes's great scenery.

It is said that the tall and dense jade laurel tree in front of the house is blooming just right, but it does not have the spirit and strength to pick up the camera and go out to leave a beautiful and moving beauty for the flower.

I dare not think about the future, because in my current situation, it will become a 1 burden wherever I go, and this is precisely what I and others cannot afford. So where can I go from here? If it be so easy to die, I don't want to live. As long as I don't leave too much trouble and burden to others and society, I am willing to take my own responsibility. Speaking of which, I couldn't help frowning again. To

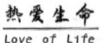
Love of Life

get rid of the predicament, I must make a breakthrough in treatment, otherwise I can only watch myself sink day by day.

I think I should agree with the doctor's proposal and try electrotherapy, which sounds very scary but is said to be very effective. So I discussed my thoughts with Neil. Neil also thinks that I should give it a try, at least there is this last hope.

Almighty God or Almighty God, please give me directions, give me a way to live full of vitality, and let me come back to life from the brink of desperation. Your old man knows that I still have a lot of beautiful scenery that I haven't taken pictures, many pretty boys and girls haven't enjoyed enough, and many delicious foods haven't had time to cook to eat! If I can Phoenix Nirvana, I will definitely not disappoint you, and I will definitely make more and greater contributions to mankind and society, believe it or not!

我与严重的抑郁症，顽强搏斗手记之一

我是二〇一八年九月初发现自己精神上出现问题的。开始我也没有太在乎，只是去看了一下普通门诊，吃点舒缓焦虑情绪的药物，但病情在几天之后急转直下，突然而来，我一下子就堕入了抑郁症的万丈深渊，不能自拔，动弹不得，如活死人一般痛苦地活着。

在经历了近一年半看不见希望，满脑子一团糟四周一片漆黑的日子，服了多种药物看了很多个医生，在沉沦中苦苦挣扎求存，我才终于看到了希望的光线和生机，生命是尊贵的，即使在求生不得度日如年的困境中，我始终都没有放弃，只要一息尚存，我就要坚持到最后一刻。

劫后余生，我今天再唱这首歌，只想告诉所有关心、帮助和爱护我的朋友：尽管抑郁症挡道，把我堕进万丈深渊，几度在死亡线上徘徊，痛不欲生挣扎求存，但我毕竟还活着，现正在康复的路上，即便前面还有很长的路要努力走下去，我也义无反顾，无怨无悔，因为生命是尊贵的，生命受之于父母，为了父母的养育之恩，我必须勇敢地活下去！我知恩并感激朋友们一路上的爱心、鼓励与相伴，因为人间有情有爱，有诗与远方，这就是我活下去的勇气与信心。

病中，我曾经看不懂一个字，说不出一句话，不会打电话和接电话，不能定神看电视、不能阅读、不能打字，甚至不能和任何人进行话语沟通，生活不能自理，连去医院填的普通病历也要别人帮忙填，想出去买一条面包也做不到，刚出门下完楼梯，就迷失了方向，找不到回家的路。到了商场在货架上呆呆站着就是看不清眼前是什么物品，更不知道自己想做什么要买什么，脑子完全是瘫痪的状态。

我感觉自己可能已经疯掉了，抗抑郁症药物的副作用更令我大小便失禁，令我常常一周时间用尽仅有的一点力气，也排不出便，低血压，一站起来就立马晕眩，眼前直冒金星，有一天病急被呼叫救护车送院急救，结果在送院急救后刚出院，就在医院门前直接晕倒在硬水泥地上，头部直接落地，跌到满脸鲜血，血肉模糊，额头破了，脸庞被撕裂了两道长长的口子，眼镜断裂，划破了鼻梁和鼻翼，嘴唇上失去一大块肉，肿成一只大猪嘴，破相成了血淋漓的丑八怪，我简直被这飞来的横祸惊呆了，倒地几分钟后，我才慢慢苏醒过来，拿出手帕擦满了一帕的鲜血，护士见状立马又把我送入医院清洗血污，医生决定要我二十四小时留院察看。

医院里有许多吸毒和酗酒的病人，夜里在病房里呻吟叫喊，鬼哭狼嚎，令我不安的心更加火上浇油，完全失去控制，一夜无眠，每分每秒都如热锅上的蚂蚁苦不堪言，但没法用语言和护士沟通，护士问来问去，我没法说话，我只有用惊恐的眼神告诉她，我无法与她沟通。

莫名其妙的焦虑情绪，令我失去对身心的控制，对一切事情都失去兴趣和信心，身体和背部像一张被拉满的弓箭，神经无法放松和休息，我甚至连自己最喜欢的写作、摄影、上网、唱歌、做饭、运动等等也动弹不得，每天二十四小时都瘫在床上盯着天花板，脑子中眼睛里都是看不见任何希望的悲观，每分每秒都是如滚针毡的煎熬，我的抑郁症复发之初医生用药不当，加深了我的病情，更拖延了我病情受到控制和好转的时机。

　　病中，我走路没有力气，一点气魄都没有，身体机能如瘫痪在床的病人，幸亏有位老同学 Shelina 由遥远的墨尔本给我寄来许多汤料、有老同学 Grace 给我邮寄茶叶和药物，有悉尼的老同学 Cathy 给我寄来营养素，还有老同学静甚至要由中国过来带我回国治疗，并让我不要担心来去经济问题，还有朋友主动联系过来澳洲照顾我，很多微信朋友更是每天都发信息和留言安慰和鼓励，列举许多坚持服药和锻炼得以康复的病例，给我面对顽疾的信心和勇气……患难见真情，这一切，使我真切感受到人间真情流露的温暖，使我在最困难的时候也没有选择放弃，特别是我爱人尼尔，在我发病和生命危在旦夕的时候，一直不离不弃地陪伴、照顾在我左右，这样的真爱与友谊，是我生命的烛光，照亮了我在茫茫汪洋大海中挣扎求存的身心，每当想起这些，我感到自己非常幸运，如果我在病中没有这些爱与关怀，陪伴与鼓励，支持与善行，我恐怕早就离开了这个世界。

　　诚然，许多朋友都不明白什么才是真正的抑郁症，在这里请允许我向大家解释一下：其实抑郁症不是一种简单的情绪化感觉，而是一种非常恐怖的，随时可以夺人性命的疾病。因为当一个人患上抑郁症，这个病就能够完全控制这个病人的思想和行为：让人脑子功能和身体功能同时瘫痪，令病者像脑子瘫痪一样失去了思考的能力，身体功能也同时瘫痪，无法动弹，让人像一个行尸走肉一样活着，严重如我者，四周漆黑一片，看不见任何光亮，想挣扎没有力气，想思考脑袋混乱不听使唤记忆断路，每分每秒都如坐针毡皮肤仿佛被无数支针刺进肉里，备受煎熬，求生不得求死不能，以致不少患者最后都忍受不了这十分磨人磨心的痛苦，无法与人沟通而选择了离开。

热爱生命
Love of Life

  所以,在我康复的路上,我希望自己能够把这段艰难的患病和康复历程记录下来,让朋友们深入了解和理解抑郁症,日后时刻警惕抑郁症的袭击,时刻保持身心健康,唯有这样我们才能够获得最大的幸福与快乐。对于已经患有抑郁症的朋友,我想你也知道,这种病是可以治疗和康复的,所以我们并不孤单,无论发生什么情况,只要我们不惊慌失措,只要我们坚持看医生按时服药,只要我们坚持锻炼身体,不放弃生命,只要我们咬紧牙关坚持到底,就一定能够渡过难关重拾自信,像我这样,现在已经在逐步好转和康复之中。

  如果你不幸也患上抑郁症,加强运动是必需的,唯有这样才会有可能看见希望的光线,才称得上爱惜生命珍惜健康。

  我们宝贵的生命受之于父母,养育于父母的含辛茹苦,我是舍不得也必然不会放弃生命的。

  此时此刻我一个人在阳光下踢足球,挥汗如雨,气喘吁吁,我不禁喃喃自语:你姥姥的抑郁症,你马上给老子滚出来,特么我一脚就把你踢到爪哇国去!

二月十五至十六日

一个抑郁症患者的手记
Notes of a depressed patient

I struggle with severe depression, tenacious notes 1

It was and early September 2008 that I discovered that I had mental problems. At first, I didn't care too much. I just went to the general clinic and took some drugs to relieve anxiety. But after a few days, my condition took a turn for the worse. Suddenly, I fell into the abyss of depression. I couldn't extricate myself and couldn't move. I lived like the living dead.

After nearly a year and a half when I could not see hope, my mind was full of chaos and dark days, I took a variety of drugs, saw many doctors, and struggled to survive in the sinking, I finally saw the light of hope and vitality. Life is noble. Even in the predicament of not being able to survive, I never gave up. As long as I have a breath, I will stick to it until the last moment.

After the disaster, I sang this song again today, just to tell all my friends who care about, help and love me: although depression got in the way, me into the abyss, wandering on the death line several times, struggling to survive, I am still alive after all, and now on the way to recovery. even if there is still a long way to go, I have no regrets, because life is noble, life by the parents, in order to raise the parents of grace, I must be brave to live! I know kindness and appreciate the love, encouragement and companionship of my friends along the way, because there is love, poetry and distance in the world, which is my courage and confidence to live.

During my illness, I used to be unable to understand a word, unable to say a word, unable to make or answer the phone, unable to watch TV, unable to read, unable to type, unable to communicate with anyone, unable to take care of myself, even the ordinary medical records filled in by others to help fill in. I couldn't go out and buy a loaf of bread. As soon as I went down the stairs, I lost my way and couldn't find my way home. When I got to the mall and stood on the shelf, I couldn't see what was in front of me, let alone what I wanted to do or buy. My brain was completely paralyzed.

I feel that I may have gone crazy. The side effects of antidepressants make me incontinent. I often use up only a little strength in a week, and I can't discharge my stool. I have low blood pressure. When I stand up 1, I feel dizzy immediately. Venus is shining in front of me. One day, I was called an ambulance to be sent to the hospital for emergency treatment. As a result, I was just discharged from the hospital after being sent to the hospital for emergency treatment, in front of the hospital, he fainted directly on the hard concrete floor. His head fell directly to the ground, his face was covered with blood, bloody, his forehead was broken, his face was torn with two long holes, his glasses were broken, his nose bridge and alar were cut, his lips lost 1 large pieces of meat, his was swollen and into a big pig's mouth, and his was and bloody ugly. I was simply shocked by this flying disaster, after falling to the ground for a few minutes, I slowly woke up, took out my handkerchief and wiped the 1 Pa's blood. The nurse immediately sent me to the hospital to clean the blood. The doctor decided to keep me in the hospital for 24 hours.

There are many patients who take drugs and alcohol in the hospital. They moan and shout in the ward at night, crying and howling, which makes my uneasy heart even more angry. They are completely out of control and have no sleep all night. They are like ants on a hot pan. However, they can't communicate with the nurse in words. The nurse asks and asks. I can't speak. I have to tell her with frightened eyes that I can't communicate with her.

The inexplicable anxiety made me lose control of my body and mind, and lost interest and confidence in everything. My body and back were like a full bow and arrow. My nerves could not relax and rest. I could not even move my favorite writing, photography, surfing the Internet, singing, cooking, sports and so on. I collapsed in bed and stared at the ceiling 24 hours a day, in my mind, my eyes are full of pessimism that can't see any hope. Every minute and second is like the suffering of rolling needle felt. At the beginning of my depression relapse, the doctor's improper medication deepened my condition and delayed my condition. The opportunity to be controlled and improved.

During my illness, I had no strength to walk and no boldness of vision. My body function was like a paralyzed patient in bed. Fortunately, an old classmate sent me many soup materials from Melbourne Shelina, an old classmate Grace sent me tea and medicine, an old classmate Cathy from Sydney sent me nutrients, and an old classmate Jing even sent me back to China for treatment, and let me not worry about the economic problems, and some friends take the initiative to contact Australian to take care of me. Many WeChat friends even send messages and messages to comfort and encourage me every day, listing many cases that persist

热爱生命
Love of Life

in taking medicine and exercise to recover, giving me confidence and courage to face stubborn diseases... All these make me truly feel the warmth of the true feelings in the world, I didn't choose to give up in the most difficult time, especially my lover Neil, who accompanied and took care of me when I was ill and my life was in danger. Such true love and friendship are the candlelight of my life and illuminate my body and mind struggling to survive in the vast sea. Whenever I think of these, I feel very lucky. If I don't have such love and care in my illness, accompany and encouragement, support and good deeds, I am afraid I have long left this world.

Admittedly, many friends do not understand what is the real depression, here please allow me to explain to you: in fact, depression is not 1 a simple emotional feeling, but 1 a very terrible, can take people's lives at any time disease. Because when a person suffers from depression, the disease can completely control the patient's thoughts and behaviors: it paralyzes the brain function and body function at the same time, making the patient lose the ability to think like a brain paralysis, and the body function is also paralyzed at the same time., Unable to move, let people live like a walking corpse, as serious as me, surrounded by darkness, can't see any light, want to struggle without strength, if you want to think about the chaos in your head and don't listen to the memory circuit, you are on pins and needles every minute and every second. skin seems to have been pierced by countless needles. You are suffering, and you can't survive. As a result, many patients can't stand the pain of grinding people's, grinding heart, unable to communicate with others and choose to leave.

Therefore, on my way to recovery, I hope I can record this

difficult illness and recovery process, so that my friends can have a deep understanding and understanding of depression, always be alert to the attack of depression in the future, and always maintain physical and mental health. Only in this way can we obtain the greatest happiness and happiness. For friends who have already suffered from depression, I think you also know that this disease can be treated and recovered, so we are not alone. No matter what happens, as long as we don't panic, as long as we insist on seeing a doctor and taking medicine on time, as long as we insist on exercising and not giving up our lives, as long as we bite the bullet and stick to it, we will be able to tide over the difficulties and regain confidence, like me, now it is gradually improving and recovering.

If you are unfortunately also suffering from depression, it is necessary to strengthen exercise. Only in this way can you see the light of hope and cherish life and health.

Our precious life by the parents, raised by the parents of the hardships, I am reluctant and will not give up life.

At this moment, I am playing football alone in the sun, sweating like rain and panting. I can't help muttering to myself: your grandmother's depression, you should roll out to Lao tze immediately, I 1 my feet and kick you to Java!

5 to 16 February

热爱生命
Love of Life

我与严重的抑郁症，顽强搏斗手记之二

　　生命乃是一首悲欢交织的歌，即使抑郁了、跌倒了、失声了、血肉模糊奄奄一息，漆黑一片挣扎着，我也要努力咬牙爬起来，擦亮自己的心灯，迈出沉重的脚步，像鹰与浴火凤凰的重生，把生命的几许风雨吟唱成绯红色的诗句，把人生的真挚与美善，坚忍与不屈，唱满一路的爱歌！

　　我从来没有想到，抑郁近一年半的日子里，我竟然连手机拍照也不会，还有什么比完全做不了自己热爱的事情更令人痛苦和泄气的呢？不少朋友在微信上信息我晒照片，所以当我此刻能够再次拿起手机为自己拍下这些家门口肉桂树的照片，我的心充满了喜悦与感激，上苍有好生之德，我佛大慈大悲，怜悯我的苦痛竟然悄悄地将我由死神的手上解救了我垂危的生命。

　　我的抑郁症非常严重，因为服量大的药才能有效控制，所以服药后副作用很多，此时此刻我拿手机拍照的手颤抖不已，平时拿筷子刀叉吃饭也颤抖不已，想定格好照片确实十分不容易，希望以后减量服药副作用能够少点，这样我拍照才能够更容易一些，无论如何，现在能够用手机拍照已经是上天对我的恩赐了，所以此时此刻我已经感到很开心。

　　一大早醒来，读着朋友们在微信的留言，我的心温暖而舒畅。感谢大家用你的心点赞，用你的爱留言，让我知道你来过，在我康复的路上，你的爱与鼓励，就在我的身边，给我活

下去的勇气和力量。

　　记得当我抑郁症病重的时候，我每天只能咬两口白面包，吃两口饭，慌乱的身心每分每秒都被病魔折磨与控制，我好像被别人扔进无边无际的茫茫大海中央，脑子的思维被残酷夺走和歪曲，不知哪里来的许多奇怪和恐怖的念头，不能够思考，手脚不能动弹，气若游丝，反抗是完全不可能的，因为除了脑袋瘫痪不能用，身体其他功能也是瘫痪的，希望更是渺茫，我唯一能做到的就是闭上眼睛任由它折磨，但只要我一息尚存，我就绝不放弃生命，直到生命的最后一刻！

　　病好转后，我领悟到，当一个人发觉自己精神不对时，应该马上去看医生，并按照医生的指导坚持按时服药，我这次由看普通门诊到心理专科，再由紧急救助到精神病理专家，开始时药都不对收效甚微并使病情加重，先后换了很多种药物，看了很多个医生，最后才知道应该找"精神科病理专家"看病服药，才能有效控制病情，接受最适合的治疗方法，配合每天不间断的身体锻炼，耐心等待身体的逐步恢复。

　　除此以外，抑郁症患病时，身边的亲人照料和支持是非常重要的，诚然，抑郁症患者及其家人也一同接受人生的挑战与煎熬，一样无助与束手无策，和病人一起经受着最艰苦的精神考验，因为这种病病情反反复复，时好时坏变化多端令人苦不堪言不胜困扰，而病人也无法与家人沟通解释抑郁症的真情实感，家人们往往除了陪病人看医生做饭洗衣照料，都眼睁睁看着病人苦苦挣扎，不能吃、不能坐、不能睡、不能看、不能读也不能写，却无力帮助减轻其痛苦，所以也一同忍受着常人难以明白的无能为力的痛苦与泪流。不管如何，病中我有爱人尼尔一直在我身边，我是十分幸运的，有尼尔的贴心关怀与照顾是令人安慰的，没有尼尔我一定已经支撑不来这么久。我很感激尼恩这一路上给我的这份深爱鼓励与支持照料！可以说我的命是他拼命帮助我捡回来的。

当然，我也衷心感谢微信和每篇所有在病中给予我鼓励留痕的朋友，同时非常欢迎有相似经历的朋友也来分享你患病及恢复的过程与感受，让我们不会感到恐惧与孤单，不会感到绝望与无助！

二月十七日

我一直热爱唱歌，可惜抑郁后我失声了一年多时间，一句话也发不了声，痛苦可想而知，但是只要我还能够发出一点声音，我就要一直歌唱着飞翔，飞翔着歌唱。

今天元宵节，辞旧迎新，祝福朋友们元宵节快乐。过了今天我们的人生就是全新的章节了，再一次感谢所有关心和爱护我的朋友和亲人，没有你们，就没有重获新生的我，你们是爱是情、是暖、是燕子梁间的呢喃，是春水的欢唱，是我活着的勇气，你们就是我人间的四月天！

我们选择了快乐，快乐就在我们心中落地生根，我们都要好好地活着，活出阳光与淡淡的花香。

昨夜星辰昨夜星，生命有些深谷，跨过了就是天堂，沉没了就是地狱，只要我们选择了顽强求生，就会在最黑暗和绝望中，获得爱的拥抱与柳暗花明又一村的灿烂与光明。

二月十八至十九日

I struggle with severe depression, tenacious notes 2

Life is a song of joys and sorrows. Even if I am depressed, fall down, lose my voice, bloody and dying, and struggling in darkness, I will try my best to grind my teeth to get up, polish my heart lamp, and take heavy steps, like the of a eagle and the rebirth of a phoenix, singing the wind and rain of life into crimson poems, and the sincerity and beauty of life into good, perseverance and perseverance, sing all the way love song!

I never thought that in the nearly one and a half years of depression, I could not even take pictures with my mobile phone. What is more painful and discouraging than not being able to do what I love at all? Many friends posted photos of me on WeChat, so when I was able to pick up my mobile phone again to take photos of the cinnamon trees in front of my house, my heart was full of joy and gratitude. God has the virtue of living well. I am Buddha with great compassion and pity. My pain quietly saved my dying life from the hands of death.

My depression is very serious, because it can be effectively controlled by taking a large amount of medicine, so there are many side effects after taking medicine. At this moment, my hand taking photos with my mobile phone trembles, and I usually trembles when eating with chopsticks, knives and forks. It is really not easy to good photos in the format. I hope that the side effects of taking medicine can be reduced in the future, so that I can take photos more easily. Anyway, now being able to take pictures with my mobile phone is a gift from heaven, so I feel very happy at this moment.

Waking up early in the morning and reading my friends' messages on WeChat, my heart was warm and comfortable. Thank you for praising with your heart and leaving a message with your love to let me know that you have been here. On my way to recovery, your love and encouragement are by my side, giving me the courage and strength to live.

I remember when I was seriously depressed, I could only bite two bites of white bread and eat two bites of rice every day. My flustered body and mind were tortured and controlled by the disease every minute and every second. I seemed to be thrown into the middle of the boundless sea by others. My mind was cruelly taken away and distorted. I don't know where many strange and horrible thoughts came from. I can't think, my hands and feet can't move, and I feel like a gossy, resistance is completely impossible, because in addition to the paralysis of the head, other functions of the body are also paralyzed, and the hope is even slimmer. The only thing I can do is to close my eyes and let it torture me, but as long as I am alive, I will never give up my life until the last moment of my life!

After the illness got better, I realized that when a person found himself mentally wrong, he should go to see a doctor immediately and take medicine on time according to the doctor's guidance. This time, I went from general outpatient to psychological Junior College, and then from emergency rescue to psychiatrist. At the beginning, medicine was wrong and had little effect and aggravated the illness. I changed many kinds of drugs and saw many doctors, finally, we know that we should find a "psychiatric pathologist" to see a doctor and take medicine, so as to effectively control the disease, accept the most suitable treatment method, cooperate with daily uninterrupted physical exercise, and wait patiently for the gradual recovery of the body.

In addition, when depression is sick, the care and support of relatives around is very important. It is true that patients with depression and their families also accept the challenges and sufferings of life together. They are just as helpless and helpless. They go through the most difficult mental test with the patients, because the disease is repeated, and the changing of good and bad makes people miserable and troubled, and the patients can't communicate with their families to explain the true feelings of depression, in addition to accompanying patients to see doctors, cook, wash and take care of them, family members often watch patients struggling, unable to eat, sit, sleep, watch, read or write, but unable to help alleviate their pain. therefore, they also endure the pain and tears of powerlessness that ordinary people cannot understand. In any case, I have my lover Neil who has always been by my side during the illness. I am very lucky. It is comforting to have Neil's intimate care and attention. I would not have been able to support it for so long without Neil. I am very grateful to Nene for the love, encouragement and support and care he gave me along the way! It can be said that he desperately helped me get my life back.

Of course, I also sincerely thank WeChat and all the friends who gave me encouragement and left marks in my illness. At the same

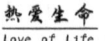
Love of Life

time, friends with similar experiences are very welcome to share your illness and recovery process and feelings, so that we will not feel fear and loneliness, despair and helplessness!

February 17

I have always loved singing, but unfortunately I lost my voice for more than a year after depression, and I couldn't say a word. The pain can be imagined, but as long as I can make a little sound, I will always sing and fly, fly and sing.

Today's Lantern Festival, farewell to the old and welcome the new, wish friends a happy Lantern Festival. After today, our life is a brand-new chapter. Once again, I would like to thank all my friends and relatives who care about and love me. Without you, I would not have been reborn. You are love and love, warm, swallows the whisper between Liang and, the singing of spring water, my courage to live, and you are the April day on my earth!

We have chosen happiness, and happiness takes root in our hearts. We all need to live well and to sunshine and faint fragrance of flowers.

Last night's stars last night's stars, there are some deep valleys in life, crossing is heaven, sinking is hell, as long as we choose to survive tenaciously, we will get the embrace of love and the brilliance and light of another village in the darkest and despair.

February 18–19

我与严重的抑郁症,顽强搏斗手记之三

  古罗马斗兽场,我仿佛耳闻目睹旧日殊死搏斗的喧嚣,生命的斗士,都必须经历血与火的洗礼,刀光剑影,生离死别,是君子,必能置之死地而重生。缅怀、凝望、感叹,人类历史的长河星光璀璨,古人来者,念天地之悠悠,独怆然而微笑!

  美不胜收的桃花,今天开得那么任性与热烈,妖娆了春天的眉眼,流动着如诗如歌的情怀,醉了每一个人的身心。有机会我们就要去欣赏这样的美景,让人生了无遗憾。

  菲茨罗伊公园那一树一树的花开,是暖透身心的陶醉,是眼睛寻访的盛宴,是心灵渴望的雨露阳光,是永远的快乐与幸福。

  柔柔的湖水柔情万千
  我只想化作湖里一条柔柔的水草
  温柔地向你呼唤
  来吧亲爱的朋友
  我在这里等你
  在水之湄
  燃亮我的心灯
  照耀你的前路
  走向满途的青碧与花香。
  朋友来吧,亮起你动人心弦的眼睛,把你的手交给希望

的春光。

二月二十日，凯恩斯

　　醉翁之意不在酒，在于山水之间，袋鼠跳绳不在绳，在于跳脱的绳韵，在于坚持锻炼身体，我抑郁并快乐着，直到我完全康复的那一天。

　　早安，我亲爱的朋友们，早安我青翠摇摆的树木和纯蓝的晴空。

　　病了一年半，今天我终于又能够自拍嗱瑟了，早晨醒来阳光正好，吃过早餐跳完绳，忽然就心血来潮自拍几张，好开心大袋鼠我又能嗱瑟了，你喜欢现在的我吗我亲爱的朋友？

　　服药后我的手还在不停地颤抖，拿手机的手不受控制地在震荡，照片拍得不够好，很不好意思！

　　但是不管副作用如何，在我的心坎中，已经有一万个春天，在涌动与伸展蔓延开去……

　　刚才下楼去检查信箱，抬头便撞见了那一树又一树的翠绿与粉红色的花开，万朵千姿，惊艳了岁月，温柔着时光，我只愿化作蜂蝶，迎着清风翩翩起舞……

　　情是心里浮动的暗流

　　想你在举杯的时候

　　欲说还休

　　才下眉头，却上心头

　　是的，唯有草木，才有甜蜜的春心荡漾和最终的冬残岁尽，叶落归根。

二月二十一日

I struggle with severe depression, tenacious notes 3

In the Colosseum of ancient Rome, I seem to have heard and witnessed the hustle and bustle of the old life-and-death struggle. All the fighters of life must go through the baptism of blood and fire. They are gentlemen who will be reborn after death. Remembering, staring, sighing, the long river of human history is full of stars. The ancients came to read the leisurely world, only but smiling!

The beautiful peach blossom is so capricious and enthusiastic today, enchanting the eyebrows and eyes of spring, flowing with poetic feelings and intoxicated everyone's body and mind. We have the opportunity to enjoy such a beautiful scenery, let life without regret.

The blossoming of trees and trees in Fitzroy Park is a warm intoxication of the body and mind, a feast for the eyes, a rain, dew and sunshine for the soul, and eternal happiness and happiness.

The gentle lake is full of tenderness.

I just want to turn into a soft water plant in the lake

Call to you tenderly

Come on, dear friend.

I'm here waiting for you

In the water of the Mekong

Burning my heart lamp

Love of Life

Shine on your way ahead

The green towards the full road is full of and flowers.

Friends, come on, light up your touching eyes and give your hand to the spring of hope.

February 20, Cairns

The drunkard's intention lies not in wine, but in the mountains and rivers. Kangaroo skipping rope is not the rope, but in rhyme and the rope that jumps off. I am depressed and happy until the day when I fully recover.

Good morning, my dear friends, good morning I the green swaying trees and the pure blue sky.

After being ill for a year and a half, today I was finally able to take selfies. I woke up in the morning and the sun was just right. after eating breakfast and jumping the rope, I suddenly took a few selfies on a whim. I am so happy that I can take again. do you like me now, my dear friend?

After taking the medicine, my hand was still shaking, and the hand holding the mobile phone was shaking uncontrollably. The photo was not good enough. I'm sorry!

But no matter what the side effects are, there have been 10,000 springs in my heart, surging and spreading...

Just now I went downstairs to check the mailbox, and when I looked up, I saw the green trees and pink flowers, thousands of flowers, amazing the years, gentle time, I only wish to turn into bees and butterflies, dancing in the breeze...

Love is the heart floating undercurrent

Think of you in a toast

I want to talk about it

Only under the eyebrows, but on the heart

Yes, only the grass and trees, there is a sweet spring heart rippling and the final winter, the end of the, the leaves return to their roots.

February 21

我与严重的抑郁症,顽强搏斗手记之四

朝阳升起了希望的光芒,照进我蔓延葱绿的阳台,早起跳了88个绳运,坐在家中阳光灿烂的椅子上吃早餐,一位年轻的洋妹子在楼下泳池中游泳,宛如一条美人鱼般浮在波光粼粼的池上,洋紫荆花浓绿的叶子漏下细碎的金光,眼前的棕榈树翠着绿叶怡人眼睛果实累累,几只蓝绿色的小鸟在树上翻飞歌唱,仿佛此刻仍然是美丽的春天,岁月静好,我心愉悦成一块可口的蛋糕,身体轻灵如聆听理查德弹奏的《秋日的私语》。

今天和尼尔一起去茶楼喝茶,然后买了许多水果回家。市场水果很多,我就买了第一张照片那些,味道都是极其鲜美的,这些热带水果,都是附近的农民所种,价格便宜健康又环保。

再跳一会儿绳,准备坐下来享受美味的水果。

把自己喜欢吃的提子和宝云芒果清洗干净,废话不说了,迫不及待地开吃!

我真的不愧是一枚如假包换的吃货。

世界上许多人许多事,流过时间的沙流,便不再留一点痕迹。

入夜,花前月下我的思念摇摇晃晃,知否知否,你是我掌中那颗永恒不变的朱砂痣,你这嫣红欲滴的一点,乃我刻骨铭心的记忆。

二月二十二日

是的，如果我们选择了快乐，快乐就在我们的心田落地生根，开花结果，我们就可以无时无处微笑地，找到生活的信心与勇气。

当我们都老了，希望我们仍然可以这样在一起吟诗作对，我为你歌唱，你为我泡茶倒酒，我们用心倾听对方的心声，你中有我我中有你，一起抚摸对方满脸的皱纹与满头的白发，微笑地对望着，就会有柔情万种由彼此凝望的微笑中，花香满径，闪烁出慈祥厚爱的光芒。

二月二十三日

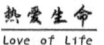

I struggle with severe depression, tenacious notes 4

The sun rose with the light of hope and shone into the verdant and balcony of my. I got up early and jumped 88 to transport the. I sat on the sunny chair at home for breakfast. 1 young foreign girl swam in the swimming pool downstairs, just like a mermaid floating on the sparkling pool. The thick green leaves of the bauhinia flower leaked the fine golden light, the palm tree in front of me is with green leaves and pleasant eyes and fruits. A few blue-green birds are flying and singing in the tree, as if it is still beautiful spring at this moment. The years are quiet and good. My heart is happy into a delicious cake. My body is as light as listening to Richard's "Autumn Whispers".

Today, I went to the teahouse with Neil for tea and bought a lot of fruit to go home. There are many fruits in the market, so I bought the first photo. The taste is extremely delicious. These tropical fruits are all grown by nearby farmers. They are cheap, healthy and environmentally friendly.

Jump a little more rope, ready to sit down and enjoy the delicious fruit.

Clean up the you like to eat, and Baoyun mango, stop talking nonsense, and can't wait to eat! I really deserve to be the 1 fake food.

Many people and many things in the world, flowing through the sand of time, will no longer leave trace.

At night, my thoughts are unsteady under the flowers and the moon. Do you know if you are the eternal cinnabar mole in my hand? Your purples are my unforgettable memory.

February 22

Yes, if we choose happiness, happiness will take root in our hearts, blossom and bear fruit, and we can smile everywhere and find the confidence and courage to live.

When we are all old, I hope we can still recite poems together like this. I sing for you, you make tea and pour wine for me, we listen attentively to each other's heart, you have me and I have you, touch each other's wrinkles and white hair all over their faces together, and look at each other with a smile, there will be tender feelings in the smile staring at each other, flowers full of fragrance, shining with kind and loving light.

February 23

热爱生命
Love of Life

我与严重的抑郁症,顽强搏斗手记之五

下雨了,窗外雨淋漓,滴滴答答,滴答滴答,织起了一张浪漫温柔的网,轻轻打在心田,随风潜入夜,润物细无声,我心的海岸温软起来,雨中想念那些爱着我喜欢着我的朋友们,满满的欢喜在心田蔓延柔然化开……

不少朋友微信我说很喜欢我的朋友圈,每天都会进来欣赏我发的内容,让我感觉到友情的愉悦与珍贵。

当你老了,你会不会也偶尔地想起我?想起在遥远的澳洲,有一只有趣的袋鼠居然患上了恐怖的抑郁症,但又奇迹般满血复活,开始整天蹦蹦跳跳了。是的,我就是这只活宝贝笔子。

其实,抑郁了又如何?既然无法痊愈,那就学会与抑郁症同行,继续活出属于自己的精彩与快乐!

二月二十四日

如果有空,让我们多去郊外走走吧,那山水那田野,那一望无际金黄色美丽的油菜花,让我们携手悠然走在过拱桥于靓丽的晴空,去拥抱曲水流觞的村庄和梦一般施施然划过的小舟,去呼吸清新怡人的天然氧吧空气,让我们愉悦陶然的身心流连忘返。

这几张是网络作品,不知道摄影师是谁,感谢他或她的出色创作,我们一起分享这养眼养心的美丽。

我终于又能够用微单相机拍照了,心中充满喜悦与激动

得泪流,唯有我知道,一年半不会拍照不能拍照的失落、无奈与悲伤,现在一切都渐渐回归正轨了,在自己家门口拍摄的感觉真幸福。

原来门口这棵开了很多粉色花的大树叫作 Cassia Javanica,中文名叫肉桂决明子树。

这场抑郁症复发让我终于领悟到:只要我们多一点爱心和善念,人间就会充满爱和温暖,我们就有希望和勇气活得更坚强和开心。

善良,的的确确是我们人类最高贵的品德。

眼前,每一朵花都是一朵美的精灵,有一种美,令人不禁静止了呼吸。

花一定是有灵魂的,因为如果我们给花以爱的滋润,用心打理,花就会在春暖的时光中恣意绽放……

二月二十五日

亲爱的朋友噢,你每天都在鼓舞着我,我也在你的鼓舞中,一天天康复起来。

知否?无论你身在何处,无论你去了何方,我永远都在这里等你,直到海枯石烂地老天荒。

我今晚入住了私家医院,浑身插满了管子,有几十条,宛如浑身被捆绑满了炸药及盒子,动弹不得,仿佛在监狱里服刑的人,其实这个是用来检测睡眠质量问题的设备,看着可怕,其实不可怕,我用了一晚上,睡得非常踏实美好。

我感动着朋友们的真挚与善良,我很幸运网络中有这样一班内涵丰富的好朋友,感恩我们的相遇,我会好好珍惜我们的友谊的。

二月二十六日

Love of Life

I struggle with severe depression, tenacious notes 5

It's raining, the rain outside the window is dripping, ticking, ticking ticking, weaving a romantic and gentle net, gently hitting the heart, sneaking into the night with the wind, moistening things silently, the coast of my heart is warm and soft, the rain misses those friends who love me and like me, full of joy spreads in the heart and softens ...

Many friends WeChat I said I like my circle of friends very much, and I come in every day to appreciate the content I send, which makes me feel the joy and preciousness of friendship.

When you are old, will you occasionally think of and me? Remembering that in the distant of Australia, an interesting kangaroo actually suffered from terrible depression, but miraculously resurrected with blood, and began to jump around all day. Yes, I am this living baby Bizi.

In fact, what about depression? Since it cannot be cured, learn to walk with depression and continue to live out your own wonderful and happy life!

February 24

If we are free, let's go to the suburbs for a walk. The mountains and rivers, the fields, the endless golden and beautiful rape flowers, let's walk hand in hand leisurely across the arch bridge in the and beautiful clear sky, embrace the villages where the water is flowing and the boats that are rowed by dreams, breathe the fresh and pleasant natural oxygen air, and let our pottery body and mind linger happily.

These are network works. I don't know who the photographer is. Thanks to his or her excellent creation, we share this beautiful beauty.

I was finally able to take pictures with a micro-single camera again. My heart was full of joy and tears. Only I knew the loss, helplessness and sadness of not being able to take pictures for a year and a half. Now everything is gradually back on track. I feel really happy to take pictures at my door.

It turns out that the big tree with many pink flowers at the door is called Cassia Javanica, and its Chinese name is cinnamon cassia tree.

This relapse of depression made me finally realize that as long as we have more love and kindness to, the world will be full of love and warmth, and we will have hope and courage to live stronger and happier.

Kindness is indeed the most noble character of our human beings.

At present, every flower is a beautiful spirit, there is a kind of beauty, people can not help but still breathe.

Flowers must have souls, because if we flowers with love and care carefully, flowers will bloom freely in the warm spring time...

February 25

Dear friend, you are inspiring me every day, and I am also recovering day by day in your encouragement.

Do you know? No matter where you are, no matter where you go, I will always be here waiting for you, until the sea withers and the rocks crumble.

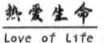
Love of Life

I was admitted to a private hospital tonight. I was covered with pipes. There were dozens of them. It was like being tied up with explosives and boxes. I couldn't move. It was like a person serving a sentence in prison. In fact, this is a device used to detect sleep quality problems. It looked terrible, but it wasn't terrible. I used it 1 nights and slept very well.

I am moved by the sincerity and kindness of my friends. I am very lucky to have such good friends with rich connotation in 1 classes in the network. I am grateful for our meeting. I will cherish our friendship.

February 26

我与严重的抑郁症,顽强搏斗手记之六

我亲爱的朋友们,我已经出院回到我美丽舒适的家了。昨天晚上,我扛着浑身插满管子的炸药包,把敌人的碉堡和自己的抑郁症彻底炸掉啦,大袋鼠我是不是非常厉害呢,哈哈!

感谢上帝,照料我的技术师洋帅哥来自悉尼,服务水平很专业,态度非常诚恳和亲切,有求必应,病房设施样样齐备和方便,住院就像住星级酒店一样令人舒适,澳洲的私家医院就是好,值得我们缴费加入服务,这样住院我感到快乐与幸福。

凯旋归来,你们的笔子仍然是个翩翩美少年!阿弥陀佛,上帝保佑我可爱的朋友们,感谢大家昨晚为我的病情担心,我现在很好,我终于又可以舞文弄墨拍照片分享嘚瑟了,让我们一起举杯同庆。来来来,葡萄美酒夜光杯,让我们开心地把这杯友谊的美酒干了。

对了,这照片中的洋帅哥有着一双英俊的深蓝色眼睛,他的名字叫作 Kelston George。

图中是我们澳洲凯恩斯库兰特的鸟世界,这些鹦鹉都不怕人,很多都飞到我们游客手中肩膀上啄食或玩耍,非常顽皮可爱。

是的,无论我身在何处,我永远是一个勇敢的中国人,我的血液里澎湃着长江与黄河,无论我说什么话,或外表有何变化,我永远都是炎黄子孙,龙的传人!

二月二十七日

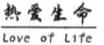
Love of Life

I struggle with severe depression, tenacious notes 6

My dear friends, I have been discharged from the hospital and returned to my beautiful and comfortable home. Last night, I was carrying an explosive bag full of pipes, blowing up the enemy's bunker and my depression completely. Is kangaroo very, ha ha!

Thank God, the technician who took care of me, Yang Shuai, is from Sydney. His service level is very professional, his attitude is very sincere and kind, and he is responsive. The ward facilities are complete and convenient. Hospitalization is as comfortable as living in a star hotel. It is good to a private hospital Australia. It is worth our payment to join the service. I feel happy and happy to be hospitalized.

Your Bizi is still a beautiful young man when you return in triumph! Amitabha, God bless my lovely friends. Thank you for worrying about my illness last night. I am fine now. I can finally take photos and share again. Let's raise our glasses together. Come on, grape wine luminous cup, let's happily dry this cup of friendship wine.

By the way, the handsome foreign boy in this photo has 1 handsome dark blue eyes. His name is George, a Kelston.

The picture shows the bird world of our Cairns Courant, Australia. These parrots are not afraid of people. Many of them fly to the shoulders of our tourists and peck at or play. They are very naughty and lovely.

Yes, no matter where I am, I will always be a brave Chinese. My blood is surging with the Yangtze River and the Yellow River. No matter what I say or what changes I have in my appearance, I will always be the of the Chinese people and the descendants of the dragon!

February 27

我与严重的抑郁症,顽强搏斗手记之七

你鼓舞了我,亲爱的。
患上忧郁症一年半,卧病在床
活着是多么艰难的混战
但我一直坚韧不拔,不放弃生命
尼尔你的爱与鼓励,鼓舞了我
我终于破茧成蝶,获得重生
我知恩并感激
还有病中每一位关心支持过我的朋友
遇见你们,是这个世界上最最动人的情真

诚然,这段漫长的日子里,如果我战胜不了自己,如果我放弃了坚韧不拔的信念,我就会像当年张国荣以及许多抑郁症患者一样,放弃生命离开了人间。

我知道我必须挣扎求存,哪怕身边是茫然一片漆黑一团,我也要勇敢地坚持下去,终于战胜了死神的挑战。

二月二十八日

I struggle with severe depression, tenacious notes 7

You inspire me, my dear.

Suffering from depression for a year and a half, bedridden

What a tough melee to be alive

But I have been tenacious and never give up life

Neil, your love and encouragement have inspired me

I finally break the cocoon into a butterfly, reborn

I know and appreciate

There are also 1 friends who care and support me during the illness.

Meeting you is the most touching love in the world.

It is true that in these long days, if I can't defeat myself, if I give up my indomitable faith, I will give up my life and leave the world like Leslie Cheung and many patients with depression.

I know that I must struggle to survive, and even if is surrounded by a blank darkness, I will bravely persevere and finally overcome the challenge of death.

February 28

热爱生命
Love of Life

我与严重的抑郁症，顽强搏斗手记之八

请让我点亮温暖如春的烛光，祝福你我的亲人朋友，你的爱与关怀，是我希望的勇气与源泉，爱你如诗初心永不改变。

西藏的林芝你就是如此的惊艳，我的眼睛与视觉都给你的美景震撼了，如此魅力非凡的姿态与色彩，教我如何不爱上你呢！

来林芝这里度假吧，这里的海水清澈见底，蓝绿色的一片又一片，碧玉似的，掬一把在手，感受透心的凉爽，尘世的喧嚣浮躁早已经没有了影踪，我已经醉倒在自然的怀抱，自然的造化仿佛天籁之音，来自天堂的巧手。

今天读到梅香依旧妹子的留言：小袋鼠你晒完美景晒美食，把馋虫都勾引出来了，美食配轻音乐，巧克力搭玫瑰，提子用纤纤玉手剥，不知道如何享受这人间美趣？想想就着急！小袋鼠一饱口福吧！替我把那一份也吃了。我不禁对着荧幕笑了。

此时此刻，我又到凯恩斯海边吹风，漫步于宁静的沙滩上，海风猎猎，感觉就像躺在妈妈的摇篮里的婴儿那般舒服，什么也不用去想，随其自然地走着，是如此的简单、平和、快乐与宁馨。

我最喜欢大海，海的声音和放牧视野的喜悦，如杯中的美酒，令人有微醺的醉意与宽心。

而海的那一端，有我的祖国，我的故乡湛江和繁荣美丽的香港和我心灵的浪漫之都珠海。

I struggle with severe depression, tenacious notes 8

Please let me light the warm candlelight, bless you, my relatives and friends, your love and care, is the courage and source of my hope, love you like poetry at the beginning of the heart will never change.

Linzhi, Tibet, you are so amazing. My eyes and vision have shocked your beautiful scenery. Such charming and extraordinary posture and color have taught me how not to fall in love with you!

Come to Nyingchi for a holiday. The sea water here is crystal clear, blue-green one after another, like jasper, holding a hand, feeling the coolness of the heart, the hustle and bustle of the world has long been gone, I have been drunk in the embrace of nature, the natural creation is like the sound of nature, the skillful hand from heaven.

Today, I read a message from Mei Xiang's sister: Small bag mouse, you bask in the perfect scene to bask in delicious food, seducing greedy insects. The delicious food is with light music, chocolate with roses, peeling with delicate hands. I don't know how to enjoy the beauty interesting in this world? Think about it and worry! Little kangaroo 1 feast! Eat that 1 for me too. I couldn't help laughing at the screen.

At this moment, I went to Cairns again to blow the wind and stroll on the quiet beach. The sea breeze hunted and hunted. I felt as comfortable as a baby lying in my mother's cradle. I didn't have to think about anything. I walked with it naturally. It was so simple, peaceful, happy and peaceful.

I like the sea best, the sound of the sea and the joy of grazing vision, such as wine in a cup, which makes people drunk and relieved.

On the other side of the sea, there is my motherland, my hometown Zhanjiang, prosperous and beautiful Hong Kong and Zhuhai, the romantic capital of my heart.

我与严重的抑郁症,顽强搏斗手记之九

三月一日,凯恩斯

十月,我的忧郁症复发,没有任何征兆,这病魔又来折磨我,我无法集中注意力做任何事情,不能阅读,不能写作,不能看电视,脑海里时常出现放弃生命的画面。我赶紧去看我的精神科专家Janet,她给我加大了药量,另外还增加了其他辅助的药物,服用到今年二月份,其间病情不上不下,好了六七成就没有进展了,于是我又陷入困境痛不欲生,基本上所有药物都无效了,我们和医生经过商讨,决定选择尝试最后一种方法,那就是电疗。

所谓电疗,就是用电疗机器由医生全身给病人麻醉后,直接通电电击病人脑部,使脑部神经产生痉挛、抽搐,从而达到治疗重度抑郁症的效果。

二月十一日,我住进了Cairns Clinic。

经过一系列的抽血检查,和医生的探讨,终于达成一致的意见,同意进行电疗。

二月二十一日进行第一次治疗,由医生James操作,每次治疗都要全身麻醉。

治疗过程很短,约莫半小时左右我就张开了眼睛,看到了护士的笑脸,她说第一次治疗很顺利完成了,我感到很高兴。

接着护士用轮椅把我推送回病房,然后给我送来了早餐:

面包，牛油和一杯热茶。

吃过早饭，我感到有点头痛和喉咙痛，后来四肢肌肉酸痛，像做了剧烈运动后的反应，护士给我吃了止痛药慢慢就不痛了。

我的爱人尼尔来医院看我，我告诉尼尔我感觉头脑清晰了，效果立竿见影，我们都很开心。

医院的精神科专家克里斯丁也和另外一位医生来看我，询问我的病况，我如实告诉她们我感觉病情好转了，她们也感到很快乐。

治疗的排期是周一，周三和周五，到今天二十六号为止，我进行了三次治疗。每做一次治疗，感觉都在好转中，所以我们都很受鼓舞。

我在医院无聊的时候就尝试看书或上网，中文书已经可以集中精神读懂一些连贯的意思了，英文书因为词语有太多生疏所以只能有个印象，这比之前一个文字都读不了好多了。

这里的护士都很友善和专业，我有事情需要解决的时候他们都乐于助人。

医院病房是酒店式的，有宽阔舒服的双人床，每天有房务员前来打扫卫生，换干净的浴巾毛巾。医院的膳食安排得挺好，厨师和服务员基本上认识每一位病人及其口味，并尽量满足大家的要求。医院有泳池和健身房，方便大家运动。还有一间艺术画廊，喜欢艺术的朋友可以进去画画和交流，我也拿起了久违的画笔。

除此，医院每周都有小组活动安排，有小组漫步、游泳、心理学和精神科治疗的理论和交流，上课的老师很友善和专业，每次参加活动我都有所收获。

我不知道还有多少次治疗才可以出院，但我已经有点迫不及待了，毕竟医院设施再好也不及自己的家来得舒服和妥帖。

因为精神集中不了很久没有写东西了，今天感觉精神状态不错，忽然就想写写自己住院的感受，试试脑袋瓜还管不管用，看来还没有完全失去功能，写到这里虽然不多，但我心里是愉快和乐观的。

我进行了第四次电疗。

这次治疗也非常顺利，电疗完吃过早餐，我已经能够在病房里看一张报纸了，我非常高兴和乐观，竟然在病房里哼起了小曲。

忽然给我做电疗的医生詹姆斯敲门进来，他和我站着进行了对话。

他问我："你现在感觉怎样？"

"非常好。"我说。

他说："好极了，既然你觉得很好，我想你今天马上就可以办理出院手续。"

"真的？"我的眼睛一定睁得贼大，我简直被这个好消息惊呆了，不敢相信自己的耳朵。

我说："这太好啦，我马上通知尼尔过来接我回家。"

十分钟后，尼尔开车飞奔而来，我俩紧紧地拥抱在一起，然后飞奔着结完账，朝着我们温暖可爱的家飞奔而去。

再见了抑郁狂魔，我老笔子胡汉三又回来啦，哈哈哈，我不禁对天大笑三声：抑郁狂魔我看你还能奈我如何？笔子我这次大难不死，脱离你的魔爪，必有后福，不信咱们就走着瞧吧！

Love of Life

I struggle with severe depression, tenacious notes 9

March 1, Cairns

In October, my depression relapsed without any signs. The disease tormented me again. I could not concentrate on doing anything, read, write or watch TV. The picture of giving up life often appeared in my mind. I hurried to see my psychiatrist Janet. She gave me more drugs and other auxiliary drugs. She took them until February this year. During this period, my illness did not go up and down. After six or seven achievements, there was no progress. So I was in trouble again. Basically all the drugs were ineffective. After discussion with the doctor, we decided to try the last 1 method, that is electrotherapy.

The so-called electrotherapy, is the use of electrotherapy machine by the doctor to the patient's body after anesthesia, direct electric shock to the patient's brain, so that the brain nerve spasm, twitching, so as to achieve the effect of the treatment of severe depression.

On February 11, I checked into the Cairns Clinic.

After a series of blood tests and discussions with doctors, they finally reached an agreement and agreed to conduct electrotherapy.

The first treatment was carried out on February 21, operated by doctor James, and general anesthesia was required for each treatment.

The treatment process was very short. I opened my eyes in about half an hour and saw the smiling face of the nurse. She said that the first treatment was successfully completed, and I was very happy.

Then the nurse pushed me back to the ward in a wheelchair and brought me breakfast: bread, butter and a cup of hot tea.

After breakfast, I felt a little headache and sore throat. Later, my limbs were sore, like a reaction after strenuous exercise. The nurse gave me painkillers and slowly stopped the pain.

My lover Neil came to see me in the hospital and I told Neil that I felt clear-headed, the effect was immediate and we were all happy.

Christian, a psychiatrist at the hospital, and 1 other doctors came to see me and asked about my condition. I told them truthfully that I felt better and they felt very happy.

The treatment schedule is Monday, Wednesday and Friday. As of today's 26th, I have had three treatments. Every time I do treatment, I feel better, so we are all very encouraged.

When I was bored in the hospital, I tried to read books or surf the Internet. Chinese books can already concentrate on reading some coherent meanings. English books can only have an impression because there are too many unfamiliar words, which is much better than the previous words.

The nurses here are very friendly and professional. They are helpful when I have something to solve.

The hospital ward is hotel-style, with a wide and comfortable double bed. Every day, a room clerk comes to clean up and change clean bath towels and towels. The meals in the hospital are well arranged. The chefs and waiters basically know every 1 patients and

Love of Life

their tastes, and try their best to meet everyone's requirements. The hospital has a swimming pool and gym, which is convenient for everyone to exercise. There are also 1 art galleries where friends who like art can go in to draw and communicate. I also picked up the brush I haven't seen for a long time.

In addition, the hospital has group activities arranged every week, including group walking, swimming, psychology and psychiatric treatment theory and communication. The teachers in class are very friendly and professional, and I have gained something every time I participate in the activities.

I don't know how many treatments are left before I can be discharged from the hospital, but I can't wait. After all, no matter how good the hospital facilities are, they are not as comfortable and appropriate as my home.

Because I can't concentrate for a long time and haven't written anything, I feel in a good state of mind today. I suddenly want to write about my feelings of hospitalization. It doesn't work to try my head. It seems that I haven't completely lost my function. Although I don't write much here, I am happy and optimistic in my heart.

I had my fourth electrotherapy.

The treatment was also very smooth. I had breakfast after electrotherapy. I was able to read a newspaper in the ward. I was very happy and optimistic and hummed a little song in the ward.

Suddenly James, the doctor who gave me electrotherapy, knocked on the door and came in. He and I stood and had a conversation.

He asked me, "How do you feel now?"

"Very good." I said.

He said, "Great, since you feel fine, I think you can go through the discharge procedures immediately today."

"Really?" My eyes must have opened a thief. I was so stunned by the good news that I couldn't believe my ears.

I said, "This is great. I'll inform Neil to pick me up and go home immediately."

Ten minutes later, Neil drove up and we hugged each other tightly, then rushed to settle the bill and headed for our warm and lovely home.

Goodbye Depressionist, my Bizi Hu Hansan is back, ha, ha, ha, I can't help laughing at the sky three times: Depressionist Demon I see you can still Nai how I am? pen me this time I will not die. If I get out of your clutches, I will have a blessing. If you don't believe me, let's see!

我的作品

My works

雄鹰之歌

我是一只雄鹰
在爱情与自由的天空中飞翔
我歌唱着飞翔
我飞翔着歌唱

如天边的云裳我来去潇洒
如胸中翻滚的诗霞
从地面我一跃而起
在广阔浩瀚的天空中
扇动钢铁的翅膀
无惧路上的风急雨狂

我振翅翱翔搏击苍穹
耳畔是呼啸风声
成又如何败又如何
云端里自由地翱翔
清风鼓起不屈的斗志
雷电爆发出诗行
流言蜚语就让它烟消云散
苦难与波折就当作生命的摇篮
刹那间掠过蔚蓝的天心

这黑色的闪电
箭一般在天空中呼啸
锐利的目光散发坚定的光芒

向上向上，再向云天的高处飞翔
我越过珠穆朗玛的高峰
翅膀在峰巅雕刻出伟岸
再飞越美丽的亚平宁
抵达英格兰俊美的海岸
然后穿越浩渺的海洋
去拥抱傲然挺立自由女神
去拥抱大洋洲宽广的蓝空

向上向上，再向更高处飞翔
没有这样的翱翔
天空也会感到寂寞与虚空
停留在空中我不禁回想
商场磨炼出斗志
金钱销蚀过诗心
爱的波折锁住了歌唱
生命在死亡边缘几度徘徊
思想与灵魂仿佛已经脱离了身体
我和严重的抑郁症作殊死的搏斗
不能自理生不如死度日如年
病中我像掉进了茫茫无际的汪洋
身旁一片漆黑没有一点光亮
看不见一丝可以生存的希望

可我毕竟是一只雄鹰
一只永不言败绝不放弃的精魂
我忍着剧痛用嘴巴拔掉身上鲜血淋漓的羽毛
我咬紧牙关坚持服药锻炼等待转机
经过一年半坚韧不拔的努力
我终于盼来了希望的曙光
挣脱了抑郁症凶狠的魔掌
雄鹰的眼睛又透出了锐光
凤凰涅槃绝地逢生
我张开了比钢铁更加坚强的翅膀

向上向上,再向高处飞翔
这不屈不挠的雄鹰
再一次在天空中奋发昂扬
翻腾展翅九万里
让一切的苦难都化作更无惧的升腾
如顺流而下的轻舟
潇风卷云送的痴狂
盘旋于浩瀚的蓝天
爆发滚烫的诗行
就让疾病和生命的波折来得更加猛烈吧
我永不言败永不放弃的信念
我熔岩喷发的激越与豪情
我要让它们永远回荡在辽阔的天空

我是一只雄鹰
在爱情与自由的天空中飞翔

我永远歌唱着飞翔
我永远翱翔着歌唱
我来自东方巨龙的故乡
我的母亲叫黄河
我的父亲叫长江
我的家在长城的脚下
我的血管奔腾着壮美的山河
我自豪我的祖国叫中国
我骄傲我是勇敢的中国人
我要为祖国的日益强盛尽情地歌唱

Song of the Eagle

I am the 1 eagle

Flying in the sky of love and freedom

I sing to fly

I fly and sing

Like the clouds in the sky, I come and go

Such as the chest rolling poetry chardonnay

I jumped up from the ground

In the vast sky

Flap the wings of steel

No fear of the wind on the road, the rain is crazy

I flapped my wings to fight the sky

Ears are the whistling wind

How to become and how to lose

Flying freely in the clouds

The wind bulges up the unyielding fighting spirit

Thunder and lightning burst into lines of poetry

Gossip makes it go away

Suffering and twists and turns as the cradle of life

In a flash, the blue heart

我的作品
My works

This black lightning

Arrows generally roar in the sky

Sharp eyes send out a firm light

Up and up, and then to the high sky of the clouds

I crossed the peak of Everest

The wings are carved on the summit.

Fly over the beautiful Apingen again

Arriving on the beautiful shores of England

And then across the vast ocean

Go embrace the Statue of Liberty

To embrace the vast blue sky of Oceania

Up, up, and then higher

No such soar

The sky will feel lonely and empty

Stay in the air I can't help but recall

Shopping malls temper fighting spirit

Money erodes the heart of poetry

Love twists and turns lock the singing

Life lingers on the edge of death several degrees

The mind and the soul seem to have separated from the body

I fought to the death with severe depression.

If you can't take care of yourself, it's better to die

Sick I like to fall into the boundless ocean

There is no light beside the dark

Can't see a glimmer of hope to survive

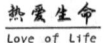
Love of Life

But I am the 1 eagle after all

1 is the spirit that never gives up.

I endured the pain and pulled out the bloody feathers with my mouth.

I clench my teeth and insist on taking medicine to exercise waiting for a turnaround

After a year and a half of hard work

I'm finally looking forward to the dawn of hope

Breaking free from the vicious clutches of depression

The eagle's eyes again showed a sharp of light.

Phoenix Nirvana, Jedi Born

I spread my wings stronger than steel

Up and up, and then fly high

This indomitable eagle

Once again in the sky

Somerset and spread 90000 miles

Let all suffering turn into a more fearless rise.

Like a canoe down the river

Xiao Feng's Crazy Send

hovering in the vast blue sky

The eruption of piping hot lines

Let the twists and turns of disease and life come more violent

I never say die never give up the faith

The excitement and pride of my lava eruption

I want them to echo in the vast sky forever

My works

I am the 1 eagle

Flying in the sky of love and freedom

I sing forever to fly

I am forever soaring singing

I come from the hometown of the oriental dragon

My mother called the Yellow River

My father called the Yangtze River

My home is at the foot of the Great Wall

My blood vessels gallop with the magnificent mountains and rivers

I am proud of my motherland called China

I am proud that I am a brave Chinese

I want to sing for the growing prosperity of the motherland

热爱生命
Love of Life

我的父母亲

　　看朱自清的《背影》时，那父亲为儿子送别情景，父爱如山，曾深深打动过我，那年三月，我刚来墨尔本留学不久，正进行紧张激烈的考试，忽然接到不幸的消息：妈妈夜里心脏病突发，家人急忙送去医院抢救，但因为是第二次发病，前后只有三小时，便离开了这个世界。

　　我心如刀割，呆呆坐在校院图书馆，窗外黄叶飘零一如我凄凉悲痛的心，轻唤一声："妈，妈妈，您怎么这样就走了？您不是答应过孩儿等我考完试回家看您的吗？"泪，默默落在桌上的书页，不相信妈妈就此永远离开了我。

　　妈妈这一走，最痛苦的莫过于失去老伴的爸爸，毕竟他和妈妈在同一屋檐下，一起生活了几十年，一辈子不知共同经历了多少风风雨雨，现在说走就走了，连一句遗言都不曾留下，怎不令老父亲孤苦无依，伤心欲绝？从此爸爸他老人家便要独对空寂的家了。

　　爸爸最放不下的是：妈妈走时他没陪伴在妈身边，他本是要送妈去医院的，但是因为年纪大行动不便，以为等妈妈病情稳定后再去不迟，不料妈妈走得这么快，这一别竟成永诀。

　　妈妈走后，爸爸整天呆呆站在窗前，他说怕妈妈的灵魂回家找不着归路，午夜梦回也总是惦记着妈，他对我说："我又梦见到你妈了，她样子很孤单，很凄凉，不知她在另一个世界可吃得饱穿得暖？病了可有人照顾？闷了可有人和她说说话儿？咱可一定要多烧些元宝纸钱漂亮干净的衣服给妈，她一贯爱美爱干净，又那么容易着凉。"父亲本是个不善言辞的男人，闻此言，我满怀酸楚。

妈妈走时我正在澳洲墨尔本念书，记得那年秋天临来澳洲前我专门由香港回家看父母，那段时间我每天去买菜，回家做饭给爸妈吃，老人家十分开心，一直不停给我说家里的故事，有时说到夜深，说到天亮，我虽然很困很困也耐心听答，我知道自己在家的日子不多，爸妈没太多要求，就只想和我多说说话，听听他们最爱儿子的声音，可惜假期很快就结束了，或许有预感，临走时一向很坚强的妈妈，竟然拥抱着我，像孩子一样哭了，我刹那间泪如雨下，连忙把年迈瘦小的妈妈抱紧。

她说："春啊，妈是七十多岁的人了，这次也许就是咱娘俩见的最后一面了，你去那么远，如果我病了山长水远的你也不用赶回来，看来我也照顾不了你了，你一个人在他乡求学，人生地不熟，会有很多困难的，孩子你可一定要自己注意身体，好好保重，吃多点东西别饿着，请你谨记一定要诚信做人，这样你的朋友就会更多，你也会因为诚信做人得到更多的发展与收获，冬天多穿件毛衣，晚上记得盖被子，要有机会就尽快找个伴，好好过诚信平实的日子……"

我不停点头，说："妈你千万别说傻话，你常说好男儿志在四方，我只是去念念书，考完试很快就会回家看你和爸爸，你俩一定要保重好身体，要不我放心不下。"

爸爸在旁听了悄悄抹泪，终于要起行了，爸爸不顾年老体弱，执意下楼送我，出租车来了，他依依不舍，秋风中一直握着我的手不放，临走还一把将我紧紧抱进怀中，久久不愿松开，直到司机催了几次他才说："孩子，祝你一路顺风。"

我坐进车里，窗外，只见爸爸的萧萧白发在风中翻飞，我刹那间泪奔禁不住又打开车门跑上前把老父亲抱紧，再亲一口爸爸慈祥的脸颊，抬头，楼上的妈妈正站在窗前，用手向我依依道别，我也向妈依依挥手，然后上车朝机场驶去。

　　妈去世的翌日，我正在考试，考完试打开电话才收到家里的消息，我马上打电话回家，准备放弃没考完的几门试回家送妈最后一程，谁知订不了机票，哥哥叫我不要着急，妈人已走，你先放心考完试再说，要不之前的努力都白费了，妈妈泉下有知也不会安息，于是我强忍悲痛把试考完，但想不到我考完试后，妈妈的遗体已经火化，我就这样错过了见妈妈最后一面。

　　第二年趁学校放假我专程回家看爸爸，没有妈妈的家已是物是人非，老父亲一见我，便伏在我的肩上放声哭了，我长这么大还是头一回见他哭得这般凄凉，撕心裂肺，他说："你妈在世时最放心不下的就是你，你一个人在外国生活，没人照料，怕你适应不了那边的气候和饮食，吃不好穿不暖，整天盼有人给你捎去些吃的用的，可那山长水远的，又能托付给谁？所以只能挂在口上，天天唠叨在想你，临住院时就担心见不着你了，要我把这枚她戴了几十年的戒指保管好，留给你作纪念。"

　　说完他由裤子的内袋，小心翼翼把那枚戒指取出给我戴上，然后微笑着摸摸我的头：春，我答应过你妈妈，一定要诚信地亲手交给你的，希望这是一个美好永恒的纪念，好好记住父母给予你的爱与温暖。

　　我在家中妈妈的灵位前为妈点上数炷香，烟雾慢慢升腾环绕着妈妈的遗照，我凝望着照片中的妈，心中默念："妈，孩儿回来看您了，您看见孩儿了吗？妈，你暖暖的掌心我摸不到，妈您到底在哪里？妈妈您干么走得这么急？妈，孩儿不孝，竟连您最后一面也见不着，最后一程也没送成，我心中不安哦妈，我知道您有多爱孩儿，可我却没向你尽到一点孝心，妈，您不知道我心中有多难过，多伤心，多惭愧，妈，我真的真的很想很想您……妈，妈，我终于学有所成，成绩优异，没有辜负你和爸爸对我的信任和期望，妈……"我跪倒在妈妈的灵前，我的泪急雨一般掉下来，掉下来……

爸爸说：妈妈临进医院时，执意把我在她生日时在香港给她买的那套高贵典雅衣服带上，所以火化时她穿的就是它。

接着我每天回家和爸爸说话，每天买许多爸爱吃的东西，买了许多新衣服给他穿上。

爸说："春啊，我都是行将入土的老人了，你还花这些钱干啥？钱留着自己防身。"可他却欢欢喜喜把新衣穿上，上次我回家时送给他的那块刻有天长地久的手表，爸一直戴着，表链子短了一点，哥说他的手腕戴肿了可他就是舍不得换下来，妈走后，爸再也不肯洗澡，他说自己应该时日无多了，到时要以妈走时的样子去见妈，容易在另一个陌生世界里相认，后来在我的劝说下爸终于肯让我帮他洗了澡，他说："好舒服。你很有孝心。"

在家一周的时间转眼便过去了，临走我去辞行，告诉爸爸我要走了，爸说："怎么这么快？你这一走，也许和上次别了妈一样，也和爸永别了，不管怎样，难得你这次千里迢迢回家看我，我很开心，我希望你在墨尔本创出一番新天地，一生都诚信对人做事，生活一定要健康快乐幸福。"

我说："爸爸您放心，我会照顾好自己，也请您多保重身体，我很快再回来看您。"

"那么我们爷俩再见啦。"我善良慈祥的爸爸，眼眶里含着依依不舍的泪光。

"嗯，亲爱的爸爸，再见啦，谢谢您和妈把我们这么多兄弟姐妹带大，我们一定会永远爱您，直到海枯石烂，地老天荒！"

在家中拥别了爸，爸这次已不能下楼送我，哥嫂把我送到楼下，抬头，爸正站在妈上次向我挥手的窗后向我挥手，此时，去年与妈道别的情景再度涌现，我心头不由得一惊：我多么担心这次又是和上次跟妈妈道别一样，一别永诀，诚然，人生最痛莫过于：树欲静而风不止，子欲养而亲不待。

今年三月，妈走了刚好四年，一生忠厚善良的爸爸在无病无痛中随妈去了天堂，接到哥哥由中国打来的电话，我握着电话和哥哥一起在线中撕心裂肺一样，失声痛哭……这是一份儿子心中永不忘怀的悲痛与哀伤！

妈走时我心中像被割去一大块肉，爸走了我的心也像被掏空了一般痛，这个世界上最无私奉献，最真心真意疼爱我的人都去了天堂，我在细雨纷飞的时节赶回家送老父亲最后一程，慈祥的爸爸走得安详，无病无痛走的，走时88岁，没有给家人带来任何的生活和经济上的负担，反而给孩子们留下了一笔舍不得用的积蓄，还有就是他一生善良、勤劳、慈爱，特别是做人做事非常诚信的高尚品德。下葬那天连天都哭了，我抚着父亲的骨灰，想起昔日父子间和睦相处的种种往事，音容宛在，父爱如山，情深似海，在纷飞的纸钱中我无限悲伤，泪水如断线的珠子默默地滚下脸颊，默默无语，依依不舍，我用手抓起一把把泥土给父亲添上，掩不住纷乱乱的心，光阴似箭，日月如梭，人生无常，红尘若梦，我无限慈祥的父亲的骨灰渐渐被泥土一点又一点，慢慢地淹没了，爸爸的骨灰终于回归永恒的大地，一切都好了，白茫茫大地一片真干净啊，纷飞的雨点，是亲情的离人泪。

我想，我或许不该来澳洲留学，这样就少了很多人生的遗憾，人往往总是在太迟的时候才醒悟过来，才懂得珍惜陪伴父母亲朋好友的可贵，人，往往在失去了才会痛心疾首，追悔莫及，这就是许多人走过的人生路程。

我在墓碑前，给墓地下长眠的爸爸妈妈深深地鞠躬，磕头，跪拜，我知道我将永远见不到也摸不着爸妈了，但我一定会牢记父母对我们的爱与温暖，特别要牢记自己无论在何时何地，都必须做一个十分诚信的，优秀的湛江人和中国人！我还在心中默念：安息吧，我最亲爱的爸爸妈妈，您俩是我心中永远的爱与痛，您俩永远活在我的心灵最深处……

就这样我回到澳洲，以诚信做人处事，快速结交了很多同样诚信的朋友，很快就在澳洲站稳脚跟，建立好自己的事业，取得圆满的成功，此外业余也在网上回归初心，重拾热爱文学摄影艺术的梦想，文思泉涌，广结善缘，创作了几百万字的文学作品并获得多个文学作品大赛一等奖和最佳作品展示奖、2个G硬盘的摄影作品，获得许多摄影比赛奖和演唱录制了389首经典歌曲，成为全民K歌签约主播，此外我还建立了《全球文学艺术精选》微信平台，担任总编辑，汇集了几千个忠实的热爱文学的活跃粉丝，还创立了《全球文学艺术精选》和《艺术精英开心乐园》两个都满员500的微信群，为热爱文学艺术，热爱生活的朋友们搭建了几个优秀的，展示才华与交流长进的平台，平实的日子过得安慰充实而有意义！

昨天再次午夜梦回，梦里依稀慈母泪，爸爸那天在湛江老家阳台上向我挥手告别……梦中父母双亲于窗前依依不舍的身影，朦朦胧胧，若隐若现，泪不知道何时已经涌进了我的眼眶，思念如影随形，蔓延进我的眼睛，十年生死两茫茫，不思量，自难忘，无处话凄凉，不知不觉，眼泪便涌出眼眶，落了下来，不能抑制，泪湿春衫……

My parents

When watching Zhu Ziqing's "Back", the father saw off his son. The father's love was like a mountain. I was deeply moved. In March of that year, I had just come to Melbourne to study and was undergoing intense exams. The news: my mother had a heart attack at night, and my family hurried to the hospital for rescue, but because it was the second time, the only three hours before and after, and left the world.

My heart ached and I sat in the library of the school. The yellow leaves fell outside the window just like my sad and sad heart. I whispered 1, "Mom, mom, why did you leave like this? Didn't you promise to wait for my child to come home to see you after the exam? "Tears, the pages that fell on the table silently, did not believe that my mother had left me forever.

The most painful thing for my mother to go this 1 is to lose his wife's father. After all, he and his mother have lived together for decades under the same roof. I don't know how many hardships and hardships they have experienced together in their whole life. Now I say I'm leaving. I didn't even leave 1 last words. Why didn't I leave my old father alone and heartbroken? From then on, my father's old man's house will be alone with the empty home.

What my father couldn't let go of was that he didn't accompany his mother when she left. He was going to take her to the hospital, but because he was too old to move, he thought it would not be too late to wait until her condition was stable. Unexpectedly, her mother walked so fast that this farewell became an eternal tactic.

After my mother left, my father stayed in the all day and stood at the window. he said that he was afraid that my mother's soul would not find a way back home. he always thought about my mother in his midnight dream. he said to me, "I dreamed of your mother again. she looked lonely and sad. I don't know if she could eat and wear warm clothes in another world? Sick but someone to take care? Is there someone to talk? We must burn more beautiful and clean clothes silver ingot paper money to mom. she always loves beauty and cleanness, and she is so easy to catch cold." My father was a man who was not good at words. I was filled with sadness when I heard this.

When my mother left, I was studying in Melbourne, the of Australia. I remember that before the came to Australia for in, I went home from Hong Kong to see my parents. During that time, I went to buy vegetables and cook for my parents every day. The old man was very happy and kept telling me stories about the family. Sometimes when it came to late at night and dawn, although I was very sleepy, listened patiently to the and answered, I know that I don't have many days at home. My parents didn't ask too much. They just wanted to talk to me and listen to their favorite son's voice. Unfortunately, the holiday was over soon. Perhaps I had a hunch that my mother, who had always been very strong when I left, hugged me and cried like a child. In an instant, I burst into tears and hurriedly hugged my old and thin mother.

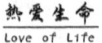
Love of Life

She said: "spring, mother is in her seventies. This may be the last time our mother and daughter will meet. If you go so far, if I am ill, the mountain the water far away, you don't have to come back. It seems that I can't take care of you either. You are studying alone in a foreign country and you are unfamiliar with your life. There will be many difficulties, children, you must pay attention to your health, take good care of yourself, eat more food, don't be hungry, please remember to be honest, so that your friends will be more, you will also get more development and harvest because of honesty, wear more sweaters in winter, remember to cover the quilt at night, find a partner as soon as possible if you have the opportunity, and live a good life of honesty..."

I kept nodding and said, "Mom, you don't say silly things. You often say that good men are determined in all directions. I just go to study. I will go home to see you and dad soon after the exam. You two must take good care of yourself, or I can't rest assured."

My father quietly wiped away his tears and finally set off. Despite his old age and infirmity, my father insisted on going downstairs to see me off. When the taxi came, he was reluctant to part with it. He held my hand in the autumn wind all the time. When he left, he to hold me tightly in his arms. He didn't want to let go for a long time until the driver urged him several times. "son, I wish you a pleasant journey."

I sat in the car and saw my father's rustling white hair flying in the wind outside the window. I couldn't help tears and opened the car door to hold my old father tightly. I kissed my father's kind cheek again and looked up. my mother upstairs was standing at the window and said goodbye to me with her hand. I also waved to my mother Yiyi and got on the bus and drove towards the airport.

My works

The day after my mother died, I was taking an exam. I didn't receive the news from my family until I turned on the phone after the exam. I called home immediately. I was ready to give up several that I didn't finish the exam. I go home and send my mother for the last time. but I couldn't book a plane ticket. my brother told me not to worry, my mother already left. you can rest assured that you will finish the exam first, or your previous efforts will be in vain, my mother knew that she would not rest in peace, so I endured my grief and finished the test, but I didn't think that after I finished the test, my mother's body had been cremated, so I missed the last time I saw my mother.

The next year, taking advantage of the school holiday, my made a special trip home to see my father. The home without my mother was a different thing. As soon as my old father saw me, he fell on my shoulder and cried loudly. When I was so old, I 1't see him crying so desolate and heartbreaking. He said: "When your mother was alive, you were most worried about you. You lived alone in a foreign country and no one took care of you, I'm afraid you can't adapt to the climate and diet there, and you can't eat well and wear warm clothes. I hope someone bring you something to eat all day, but who can you entrust the mountain with long water? Therefore, I can only hang it on my mouth and nag about thinking about you every day., when I was and hospitalized, I was worried that I would not see you. I asked me to keep this ring that she had worn for decades and leave it to you as a commemorative ."

After that, he carefully the inner bag of his trousers, took out the ring and put it on me, then touched my head with a smile: spring, I promised your mother that I would give it to you with good faith. I

热爱生命
Love of Life

hope this is a beautiful and eternal memorial, and remember the love and warmth given to you by my parents.

In front of my mother's spiritual position at home, I lit and several incense for my mother's. The smoke slowly rose around my mother's photo. I stared at my mother in the photo and said to myself, "Mom, the child has come back to see you. Have you seen the child? Mom, I can't touch your warm palm, mom where are you? Mom, why are you leaving in such a hurry? Mom, my child is unfilial, and I can't even see you for the last time. I didn't get the last time. My heart is uneasy. mom, I know how much you love your child, but I didn't show you a little filial piety. mom, you don't know how sad, sad and ashamed I am. mom, I really miss you very much... mom, mom, I finally learned something, excellent grades, did not live up to you and my father's trust and expectations of me, mom... "I knelt in front of my mother's spirit, my tears fell down the rain, fell down...

Dad said: When my mother was in the hospital in, she insisted on bringing the noble and elegant clothes I bought for her in Hong Kong on her birthday, so she was wearing it when she was cremated.

Then I went home every day to talk to my father. I bought many things that my father loved to eat and bought many new clothes for him to wear.

Dad said, "spring, I am an old man who is about to be buried. why do you spend all this money? Keep the money for your own self-defense." However, he put on new clothes with joy. The watch engraved with everlasting time that I gave him when I came home last time that my father had been wearing it all the. The watch chain was a little short. My brother said that his wrist was swollen wearing it, but he just couldn't bear to change it. After my mother left, my father refused to take a bath any more. He said that he should have no more time, when the time comes, I will go to see my mother as she left. It is easy to and in another strange world. Later, under my persuasion, my father finally asked me to take a bath for him. He said, "It's very comfortable. You are very filial."

The week at home passed quickly. Before I left, I went to say goodbye and told my father that I was leaving. Dad said, "Why so fast? This 1 of you may be the same as the last time you left your mother's, and you will also goodbye to your father. Anyway, it is rare for you to come all the way home to see me this time. I am very happy. I hope you can create a new world in Melbourne. You will do things with integrity all your life, and your life must be healthy, happy and happy."

I said, "Dad, you can rest assured that I will take good care of myself and please take good care of yourself. I will come back to see you soon."

"Then we cannot father goodbye." My kind and kind father, eyes with reluctant tears.

"Well, dear father, goodbye, thank you and mom for bringing up so many of our brothers and sisters, we will love you forever, until the sea withers and the rocks crumble, the end of the world!"

I hugged my father at home. my father's could not go downstairs to see me off this time. my elder brother and sister-in-law took me downstairs and looked up. my father was standing behind the window where my mother waved to me last time. at this time, the scene of saying goodbye to my mother emerged again last year. my heart was shocked:

Love of Life

how worried I was that this time it was the same as saying goodbye to my mother last time. indeed, the most painful thing in life is that trees want to be quiet but the wind does not stop, and children want to be raised but relatives do not wait.

In March this year, my mother has been gone for just four years. My father, who was honest and kind-hearted all his life, went to heaven with his mother without any illness or pain. He received a phone call from his brother. I held the phone and cried bitterly as if I were tearing my heart and cracking my lungs online... This is the 1 grief and sorrow that my son will never forget in his heart!

When my mother left, my heart felt as if the had been cut off and 1 large pieces of meat. When my father left, my heart felt as if I had been hollowed out. The people who gave me the most selfless dedication and loved me most sincerely went to heaven. I rushed home in the drizzle season and to send old father for the last trip. The kind father walked and peacefully and. He left without illness and pain. He was 88 years old, he did not bring any life and financial burden to his family. On the contrary, he left a sum of savings that he could not bear to use. In addition, he was kind, hardworking and loving all his life, especially his noble character of being a man and doing things with great integrity. On the day of burial, I cried for days. I caressed my father's ashes and remembered all kinds of past events of harmony between father and son in the past. My voice was like a mountain of father's love and deep feeling like the sea. I was infinitely sad in the flying paper money. Tears rolled down my cheek silently like broken beads. My was silent and reluctant to part. I grabbed a handful of mud with my hand and gave my father a chaotic heart, the world of mortals is like a dream. The ashes of my infinitely kind father are gradually drowned by the mud bit by bit. My father's ashes finally return to the eternal earth. Everything is fine. The vast white earth is really clean. The swirling raindrops are the tears of family affection.

I think I probably shouldn't come to and study in Australia, so that there will be less regrets in life. People often wake up too late and know how to cherish the value of accompanying their parents, relatives and friends. People often feel sad and regret when they lose it. This is the life journey that many people have traveled.

In front of the tombstone, I bowed deeply, kowtowed and knelt down to my parents who were sleeping under graveyard. I knew that I would never see or touch my parents, but I would definitely remember the love and warmth of my parents for us, especially remember that I must be a very honest and excellent Zhanjiang people and Chinese no matter when and where I am! I still say in my heart: rest in peace, my dearest parents, you are the eternal love and pain in my heart, you live in the deepest part of my heart forever...

In this way, I returned to Australia, acted with integrity, quickly made many friends with the same integrity, and soon gained a firm foothold in the Australian, established my own career, and achieved complete success. In addition, I also returned to my original intention online, regained my dream of loving literature and photography art, and made a lot of good friends, I have created millions of words of literary works and won the first prize in many literary works competitions and the best works exhibition award, 2G hard disk photography works, won many photography competition awards and sang and recorded 389 classic songs, and became the national K song

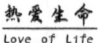
Love of Life

contract anchor. In addition, I also established the WeChat platform of "Global Literature and Art Selection" and served as the chief editor, it has gathered thousands of loyal and active fans who love literature, and has also created two full −500 WeChat groups, "Global Literature and Art Selection" and "Art Elite Happy Paradise". It is for friends who love literature and art and love life. Several excellent platforms have been built to show their talents and communicate with each other, and a plain life is comforting, substantial and meaningful!

Yesterday, I had a dream again at midnight. My mother's tears were vaguely in my dream. My father waved goodbye to me on the balcony of my hometown in Zhanjiang that day... In my dream, my parents were reluctant to part from the window, hazy and looming, tears I don't know when they have poured into my eyes. My thoughts are like shadows, spreading into my eyes. Ten years of life and death are boundless, I don't think, I don't know, I don't remember, tears gushed out of the eyes, fell down, can't restrain, tears wet spring shirt...

春风吹又生

遥远的北国冰消雪融,傲霜挺立的梅香在枝头散发阵阵的幽香,缕缕香魂跌落春水,溪水蜿蜒欢畅,快乐地流过树丛,江南青嫩的柳条,也迫不及待拂开了春天的帷帘。

经历了漫长的严冬,郊外一带的田野,已是一片又一片葱茏,绿得发亮的色彩随春风荡向天边,远山含笑,春阳暖暖,身边凋零了的树木,也不知不觉抽出春芽的柔嫩,宛如天津脆生生鸭梨的皮肤,也如西湖柳岸的新绿,大自然的神工鬼斧,雕刻剪裁,装点春天的布景,正是:不知细叶谁裁出,二月剪刀似春风。

春天从寒冬的梦中伸个懒腰,悠悠醒转,睡眼惺忪。

春风裁剪绿叶,燕子剪着春风,百灵鸟的歌音,多么清脆嘹亮,那田间的流水叮叮咚咚,想象祖国彼端的江南春水绿如蓝,那些欢跳着出笼的鸭子,是否撒开脚丫拍动翅膀扑向碧水柔凝,红掌拨着清波?喜悦清新的柔波抚得鸭子的心醉起缕缕波纹,咯咯的欢声,乃春回大地悠扬的箫音。

春风玉指轻俏,春骑漫满香痕,每一点触都化作柔凝,草坪、树木、山坡,枯木唤醒希望的种子,晨露的嫩叶,乃春天喜悦的泪珠,阳光中闪耀,楚楚莹亮。这样的春光明媚,不知有多少帅哥美眉,正怀着春心,等着春归梦里人翩临,牵手品春如酒,沐浴风流,双双醉倒于春的怀抱。

望向维多利亚海港,春风的吻是绿色的波涛,春的嘴唇吻出海面温柔的眉痕,春波凝醉,在碧海轻波中依回,诉说春来的欢欣,暖暖的阳光,浮光跃金,每一点闪烁都闪出希望,每一次跳跃都轻舞飞扬,每一个眨眼都春心荡漾。

结巢梁上的燕子,在幽秘的廊前呢喃情歌,不时翻飞的身影矫健轻盈,郊外的麻雀们,在春风中急雨般掠向天空,然后又急雨般降落春野,莫非它们要狠狠呼吸春回大地的鲜芳,或许田间还有几条肥白可口的春虫可以大快朵颐,那刚翻新的泥土油亮油亮,垂柳倒映青碧的湖岸,春风轻柔,柳絮如玉的芽儿,宛如婴孩胖嘟嘟的脸蛋,看了便想拥抱和亲吻。

一场春雨,大地洒遍甘霖,空气中处处弥漫青草的芳香,人们跃跃欲试,眼里禁不住春光乍泄,都市女子迫不及待披上春装,柔嫩的臂弯流露玉凝,袅娜的腰身曲线玲珑妖娆娉婷,俊美的男士更不遑多让,厚重的冬衣换成无袖背心,壮健的臂膀透出古色深胴,春花到处含苞待放,香港这颗美丽的东方之珠,正沐浴着如酒的春风,荡漾着千树万树的绿浪与花香。

家里的水仙花开得千姿百态,几枝桃花在开枝散叶,墨竹也越发清丽透亮,满满一个花瓶,都是春花烂漫的姿态。

我走在乡野的田埂上,身心唱着欢快的轻歌,我张开嘴巴,贪婪空气的清鲜,我禁不住张开双臂,把这春的色彩紧紧拥抱,但愿这春色绿了人间满眼,但愿这春风化去人间的忧患,但愿世间万物沐浴无边的春色与喜悦,但愿全人类都活得自由畅放,充满希望。

这几年的疫情,令我们经历了人生许多痛苦与考验,但历史经验告诉我们,野火烧不尽,春风吹又生,只要我们坚韧不拔,耐心的坚强地与疫情搏斗,我们就一定能够战胜貌似强大无比,不可一世,横行霸道的病魔,还我们一个和平安宁的天空!

春风化雨，微醺的歌音在耳畔回响，此时此刻，我指尖的文字也流淌浓浓的春意，鸟、云、月、树在春的枝头诗情画意，如墨溶于水，徐徐化开。

我们红袖杂谈，在经历了一段最低谷的无限凄迷，在六星论坛管理组紫晶总监，醉笑助理总监的英明果敢决策，以及大美丽和许多热爱红袖的朋友努力下，终于走出艰难的困境，杂谈的天空顷刻之间云雾散去，透露了蔚蓝色的丽日晴天，我们红袖杂谈的朋友们，宛如高山流水遇知音，又再一次在文字的交流中轻舞飞扬，智慧与智慧擦出的火花，心弦共颤，宛如春风化雨，滋润生命的田园，给我们在一起陪伴了快二十年的红袖深情，带来春色满园、春暖花开、花香满径。

春天带着微笑轻轻向我们走来，春风和煦的笑脸荡漾和平希望，我衷心希望我们红袖杂谈，在大美丽首版和全体版主的带领下，把我们红袖杂谈，办得春意盎然，有情有趣，舒心畅快。

热爱生命
Love of Life

Spring breeze blows again

The ice and snow melt in the far north, the plum incense stands upright with pride and frost gives out bursts of fragrance on the branches, the spirit of wisps of fragrance falls the spring water, the stream winds and merrily, flowing happily through the bushes, and the tender wicker in the south of the Yangtze River can't wait to brush open the curtain of spring.

After a long severe winter, the fields in the suburbs have become verdant one after another. The shiny green colors swinging to the sky with the spring breeze. The distant mountains are smiling, the spring sun is warm, and the withered trees around them unconsciously pull out the tenderness of spring buds, just like the skin of Tianjin crisp ppy pears, the new green on the willow bank of the West Lake, and the tricks and axes by nature, the scenery decorating spring is exactly: I don't know who cut the fine leaves, and February scissors are like spring breeze.

Spring from the winter dream stretch a stretch, leisurely awake turn, sleepy eyes.

The spring breeze cuts the green leaves, the swallows cut the and the spring breeze, the lark's song is, how clear and loud, the flowing water in the field ding ding ding dong dong dong dong dong, imagine the south of the Yangtze river spring water on the other side of the motherland is as green as blue, the ducks jumping out of the cage, whether they spread their feet and flap their wings to the clear water, soft and, red palm? Joyful and fresh soft waves caress the hearts of ducks intoxicated with ripples, giggle of joy, is the melodious sound of the spring back to the earth.

Spring breeze jade refers to light, spring riding is full of fragrant marks on the, every touch turns into soft, lawns, trees, hillsides, dead wood awakens the seeds of hope, the leaves of morning dew, is the tears of spring joy, shining in the sun, Chuchu jade-like is bright. Such a beautiful spring scenery, I do not know how many handsome boys and girls, are pregnant with the heart of spring, waiting for the dream of spring to return to people to come to the, holding hands to the of spring such as wine, bathing in romantic, both drunk in the arms of spring.

Looking at Victoria Harbour, the kiss of spring breeze is green waves, the lips of spring kiss the gentle eyebrows on the surface of the sea, spring waves and drunk, in the blue sea light waves, clinging back to the, telling the joy of spring, warm sunshine, floating light and gold, every flicker of hope, every jump dancing, every blink of an eye is spring heart rippling.

The swallows on the beam of the nest murmured love songs in front of the of the secluded corridor. The figures flying from time to time were strong and light. The sparrows in the suburbs swept to the sky like rain in the spring breeze, and then landed the spring field like rain. Would it be necessary for them to breathe hard the fresh fragrance returning to the earth in spring, perhaps there are still a few white, and delicious spring insect in the field that can be eaten. The newly

热爱生命
Love of Life

renovated soil is shiny, and the weeping willows reflect the green lake shore. The spring breeze is soft, and the catkin is like a baby's chubby face. After seeing it, I want to hug and kiss.

1 a spring rain, the earth sprinkled times of rain, the air is filled with the fragrance of grass everywhere, people are eager to try, their eyes can't help but let go of the spring, city women can't wait to put on spring clothes, tender arms reveal jade, graceful waist curve exquisite enchanting graceful, handsome men not to mention, heavy winter clothes replaced by sleeveless vests everywhere, bract color show ancient, hong Kong, the beautiful Pearl of the Orient, is bathed in the spring breeze like wine, rippling with the green waves and flowers of thousands of trees.

The daffodils in the home are blooming in various forms. A few peach blossoms are blooming and scattering leaves. The ink bamboo is becoming more and more beautiful and translucent. A vase is full of spring flowers.

I walked on the ridge of the countryside, singing cheerful light songs both physically and mentally. I opened my mouth and the clear and fresh air of greed. I couldn't help but open my arms and hug the color of spring tightly. I hope this spring color has turned the world green. I hope this spring breeze will turn away from the worries of the world. I hope everything in the world will bathe in the boundless spring color and joy. I hope all mankind live a free, and, full of hope.

The epidemic in the past few years has caused us to experience many pains and tests in our lives, but historical experience tells us that wildfires are endless and the spring breeze blows again. As long as we persevere and patiently fight the epidemic, we will definitely be able to overcome the seemingly powerful, unstoppable, domineering disease, and return us a peaceful and peaceful sky!

The spring breeze turns into rain, and the tipsy songs resound in my ears. At this moment, the words at my fingertips are also flowing with thick spring. Birds, clouds, months and trees are poetic and picturesque in the branches of spring. For example, ink dissolve in water and slowly and.

Our red sleeve miscellaneous talk, after experiencing a period of infinite sadness at the lowest point, under the wise and bold decision-making of amethyst director of the management group of the six–star forum, assistant director of drunk smile, and the efforts of great beauty and many friends who love red sleeve, we finally got out of the difficult predicament. the sky of miscellaneous talk disappeared in an instant, revealing the blue sunny day, and our friends of red sleeve miscellaneous talk were just like bosom, once again, in the exchange of words, the sparks of wisdom and wisdom, the heartstrings chatter together, just like the spring breeze and rain, moistening the countryside of life, giving us the deep feeling of red sleeves that have been with us for nearly 20 years, bringing spring colors to the garden, spring flowers and the fragrance of flowers.

Spring comes to us gently with a smile, and the warm smiling face of the spring breeze ripples with hope for peace. I sincerely hope that under the leadership of the first edition of Great Beauty and all the moderators, we can make our red sleeve talk full of spring, interesting and comfortable.

秋日的私语

秋天的叶子，宛如一个魔术师挥动的颜色魔棒，所经过的树木，色彩每天都变得梦幻，秋风拂过绯红色的广场，那些榆树的绿叶，一夜之间就变得金黄，在秋风中瑟瑟抖颤。

恼人的秋风，自顾自翻动着叶子过往，丝毫不顾叶子饱含着别离的悲伤，那些春天留下的葱茏，那些青春欢畅的时辰，夏季的爱情那样热烈沉醉的疯狂，都藏匿在叶子密密麻麻的纹路上。

然而，当秋高气爽，枫叶染红了天空的脸蛋，在透明的阳光下熠熠发光，愉悦着我们的心灵，吟诵着色彩缤纷，醉人心扉的诗行，澄净于醉人的秋光，丝毫不见就要与树木离别的悲伤，毕竟秋叶们都这样轰轰烈烈地展示过自己迷人的魅影，就算不得不别离，也没有留下什么遗憾。这和我们年轻的时候，不顾一切地去追求爱情，都一样令人欣赏和赞叹。

一对情侣在枫树下经过，他们在树下徘徊而徜徉，我在阳光灿烂的日子里，摘下几片鲜红的枫叶，回家夹在心爱的书本上，想要留下秋天的自传，以便将来再慢慢拿出来欣赏。

秋天，这美丽而动人诗篇，似微风拍响的手掌，把我的心震撼得无限欣欢。

就好像风中的叶子那样轻舞飞扬；秋天的风啊越来越疯狂，叶子在秋里枯萎却依旧迎风飘荡，哪怕即将要脱离树干翻滚在泥浆。

瞧那银杏树下已是醉人的金黄，这一片枫树也任凭它的红叶把天地尽染，一阵风吹过来，不少叶子就轻轻地飘下来，回到了地母温馨的怀抱。

不诉凄凉，零落成泥也要用心编织来春最美的轻装。

我爱这秋天里的斑斓烂漫，爱这诗情画意的秋高气爽，我爱深呼吸秋天里特有的芳香。

知道吗？我最喜欢在秋天里想你，想你的时候，这些玲珑剔透饱含哲理的诗句就会变得无比蓬勃无比盎然。

说不尽的春来夏去，秋霜冬寒，道不尽的风花雪月，儿女情长，我很固执地相信，这些色彩斑斓的秋叶，最懂得诗人缤纷的诗情。

也唯有这些动人的叶子，才愿意一片又一片，一群又一群，在我的心中翻滚而升腾，馥郁而跌宕。

热爱生命
Love of Life

Whispers of Autumn

Autumn leaves, like a magician waving a magic wand of color, through the trees, color every day become dreamy, autumn wind blowing crimson square, the green leaves of those elm trees, overnight became golden, trembling in the autumn wind.

The annoying autumn wind, turning the leaves on its own, regardless of the sadness of parting, the verdant leaves left by spring, the joyful hours of youth, the warm and intoxicated madness of love in summer, are hidden in the dense lines of leaves.

However, when the autumn is crisp, the maple leaves dye the sky's face, shine in the transparent sun, delight our hearts, recite colorful and intoxicating poems, clear in the intoxicating autumn light, and there is no sadness to leave the trees. After all, the autumn leaves have shown their charming phantom so vigorously that even if they have to leave, there is no regret left. This and when we were young, desperate to pursue love, are just as admirable and admirable.

A couple passed under the maple tree. They wandered under the tree. On a sunny day, I took off a few bright red maple leaves and went home to clip them on my beloved book. I wanted to leave an autobiography of autumn so that I could take it out slowly and appreciate it in the future.

In autumn, this beautiful and moving poem, like a breeze

clapping palm, shocked my heart to infinite and joyful.

Just like the leaves dancing in the wind; The autumn wind is getting crazier and crazier. The leaves wither in autumn but still float in the wind, even if the is about to break away from the trunk and roll in the mud.

Look at the ginkgo tree is already intoxicating golden, this maple tree also let its red leaves dye the world, a gust of wind blowing, many leaves gently float down, back to the ground mother warm embrace.

Don't complain desolate, scattered into mud also want to carefully weave to the spring the most beautiful light.

I love this autumn in the colorful romance, love this poetic autumn, I love to take a deep breath in the unique fragrance of autumn.

You know what? I like to miss you most in autumn. When I miss you, these exquisitely carved poems full of philosophy will become extremely vigorous and abundant.

The endless spring comes and summer goes, the autumn frost the winter is cold, the endless wind, flowers, snow and moon, and the love of children. I stubbornly believe that these colorful autumn leaves know best the colorful and poetry of poets.

Only these moving leaves are willing to roll and rise in my heart, 1 and 1, fragrant and ups and downs.

雕刻时光

我凝视,掌中纵横交错的阡陌
眉眼盈盈里,仿佛停止了呼吸
宇宙洪荒在地平线,一直延伸万里
或深或浅的痕迹,无可避免地别离
岸边徘徊,我,居于水湄之子
用眼睛,丈量生死,雕刻时光
雕刻时光,时光徘徊在山的另一端
雕刻人生的帆影,风平浪静
或惊涛骇浪,都暗合手中的掌纹
时光之内,那些绯红色押韵的句子
时光之外,那些超越红尘的心痴
一代又一代,生生不息
时光在白沙滩岸边写着落红的诗
我越过晚霞的光线
用眼睛拥抱天堂里最亲爱的你
我俩这段为爱痴狂的爱情
光照日月超越生死
刻骨铭心永不忘记
就这样一辈子与你相依
我在时光的白沙滩岸边流连再流连
情到深处涌出相思

我以思念雕刻时光

唇端滑落一首,白沙滩上绵延的宋词

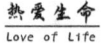

Carving Time

I stare, the criss-cross fields in the palm of my hand
Eyebrow eyes in, as if to stop breathing
The universe is on the horizon, stretching for thousands of miles
Or deep or shallow traces, inevitably parting
Wandering on the shore, I, the son of the Mae who live in the water
With eyes, measuring life and death, carving time
Carving time, time hovers at the other end of the mountain
Sculpture the life of the sail shadow, calm
Or stormy waves, all of which fit the palm print in your hand
In time, those crimson rhyming sentences
Outside of time, those hearts beyond the world of mortals
Generation after generation, endless
Time is writing a red poem on the bank of the white sand beach
I crossed the sunset light
Embrace the dearest you in heaven with your eyes
This crazy love between us
The sun and moon shine beyond life and death
Never forget
In this way, I will depend on you all my life
I am in the time of the white sand beach shore again

我的作品
My works

Love to the depths of the lovesickness

I miss the carving time

A song slipped from the lip end, and the Song lyrics stretched on the white sand beach

www.ingramcontent.com/pod-product-compliance
Lightning Source LLC
Chambersburg PA
CBHW071233070526
44583CB00017B/2164